All Things Considered

by

G. K. Chesterton

CONTENTS

THE CASE FOR THE EPHEMERAL

I cannot understand the people who take literature seriously; but I can love them, and I do. Out of my love I warn them to keep clear of this book. It is a collection of crude and shapeless papers upon current or rather flying subjects; and they must be published pretty much as they stand. They were written, as a rule, at the last moment; they were handed in the moment before it was too late, and I do not think that our commonwealth would have been shaken to its foundations if they had been handed in the moment after. They must go out now, with all their imperfections on their head, or rather on mine; for their vices are too vital to be improved with a blue pencil, or with anything I can think of, except dynamite.

Their chief vice is that so many of them are very serious; because I had no time to make them flippant. It is so easy to be solemn; it is so hard to be frivolous. Let any honest reader shut his eyes for a few moments, and approaching the secret tribunal of his soul, ask himself whether he would really rather be asked in the next two hours to write the front page of the *Times*, which is full of long leading articles, or the front page of *Tit-Bits*, which is full of short jokes. If the reader is the fine conscientious fellow I take him for, he will at once reply that he would rather on the spur of the moment write ten *Times* articles than one *Tit-Bits* joke. Responsibility, a heavy and cautious responsibility of speech, is the easiest thing in the world; anybody can do it. That is why so many tired, elderly, and wealthy men go in for politics. They are responsible, because they have not the strength of mind left to be irresponsible. It is more dignified to sit still than to dance the Barn Dance. It is also easier. So in these easy pages I keep myself on the whole on the level of the *Times*: it is only occasionally that I leap upwards almost to the level of *Tit-Bits*.

I resume the defence of this indefensible book. These articles have another disadvantage arising from the scurry in which they were written; they are too long-winded and elaborate. One of the great disadvantages of hurry is that it takes such a long time. If I have to start for High-gate this day week, I may perhaps go the shortest way. If I have to start this minute, I shall almost certainly go the longest. In these essays (as I read them over) I feel frightfully annoyed with myself for not getting to the point more quickly; but I had not enough leisure to be quick. There are several maddening cases in which I took two or three pages in attempting to describe an attitude of which the essence could be expressed in an epigram; only there was no time for epigrams. I do not repent of one shade of opinion here expressed; but I feel that they might have been expressed so much more briefly and precisely. For instance, these pages contain a sort of recurring protest against the boast of certain writers that they are merely recent. They brag that their philosophy of the universe is the last philosophy or the new philosophy, or the advanced and progressive philosophy. I have said much against a mere modernism. When I use the word "modernism," I am not alluding specially to the current quarrel in the Roman Catholic Church, though I am certainly astonished at any intellectual group accepting so weak and unphilosophical a name. It is incomprehensible to me that any thinker can calmly call himself a modernist; he might as well call himself a Thursdayite. But apart altogether from that particular disturbance, I am conscious of a general irritation expressed against the people who boast of their advancement and modernity in the discussion of religion. But I never succeeded in saying the quite clear and obvious thing that is really the matter with modernism. The real objection to modernism is simply that it is a form of snobbishness. It is an attempt to crush a rational opponent not by reason, but by some mystery of superiority, by hinting that one is specially up to date or particularly "in the know." To flaunt the fact that we have had all the last books from Germany is simply vulgar; like flaunting the fact that we have had all the last bonnets from Paris. To introduce into philosophical discussions a sneer at a creed's antiquity is like introducing a sneer at a lady's age. It is caddish because it is irrelevant. The pure modernist is merely a snob; he cannot bear to be a month behind the fashion Similarly I find that I have tried in these pages to express the real objection to philanthropists and have not succeeded. I have not seen the quite simple objection to the causes advocated by certain wealthy idealists; causes of which the cause called teetotalism is the strongest case. I have used many abusive terms about the thing, calling it Puritanism, or superciliousness, or aristocracy; but I have not seen and stated the quite simple objection to philanthropy; which is that it is religious persecution. Religious persecution does not consist in thumbscrews or fires of Smithfield; the essence of religious persecution is this: that the man who happens to have material power in the State, either by wealth or by official position, should govern his fellow-citizens not according to their religion or philosophy, but according to his own. If, for instance, there is such a thing as a vegetarian nation; if there is a great united mass of men who wish to live by the vegetarian morality, then I say in the emphatic words of the arrogant French marquis before the French Revolution, "Let them eat grass." Perhaps that French oligarch was a humanitarian; most oligarchs are. Perhaps when he told the peasants to eat grass he was recommending to them the hygienic simplicity of a vegetarian restaurant. But that is an irrelevant, though most fascinating, speculation. The point here is that if a nation is really vegetarian let its government force upon it the whole horrible weight of vegetarianism. Let its government give the national guests a State vegetarian banquet. Let its government, in the most literal and awful sense of the words, give them beans. That sort of tyranny is all very well; for it is the people tyrannising over all the persons. But "temperance reformers" are like a small group of vegetarians who should silently and systematically act on an ethical assumption entirely unfamiliar to the mass of the people. They would always be giving peerages to greengrocers. They would always be appointing Parliamentary Commissions to enquire into the private life of butchers. Whenever they found a man quite at their mercy, as a pauper or a convict or a lunatic, they would force him to add the final touch to his inhuman isolation by becoming a vegetarian. All the meals for school children will be vegetarian meals. All the State public houses will be vegetarian public houses. There is a very strong case for vegetarianism as compared with teetotalism. Drinking one glass of beer cannot by any philosophy be drunkenness; but killing one animal can, by this philosophy, be murder. The objection to both processes is not that the two creeds, teetotal and vegetarian, are not admissible; it is simply that they are not admitted. The thing is religious persecution because it is not based on the existing religion of the democracy. These people ask the poor to accept in practice what they know perfectly well that the poor would not accept in theory. That is the very definition of religious persecution. I was against the Tory attempt to force upon ordinary Englishmen a Catholic theology in which they do not believe. I am even more against the attempt to force upon them a Mohamedan morality which they actively deny.

Again, in the case of anonymous journalism I seem to have said a great deal without getting out the point very clearly. Anonymous journalism is dangerous, and is poisonous in our existing life simply because it is so rapidly becoming an anonymous life. That is the horrible thing about our contemporary atmosphere. Society is becoming a secret society. The modern tyrant is evil because of his elusiveness. He is more nameless than his slave. He is not more of a bully than the tyrants of the past; but he is more of a coward. The rich publisher may treat the poor poet better or worse than the old master workman treated the old apprentice. But the apprentice ran away and the master ran after him. Nowadays it is the poet who pursues and tries in vain to fix the fact of responsibility. It is the publisher who runs away. The clerk of Mr. Solomon gets the sack: the beautiful Greek slave of the Sultan Suliman also gets the sack; or the sack gets her. But though she is concealed under the black waves of the Bosphorus, at least her destroyer is not concealed. He goes behind golden trumpets riding on a white elephant. But in the case of the clerk it is almost as difficult to know where the dismissal comes from as to know where the clerk goes to. It may be Mr. Solomon or Mr. Solomon's manager, or Mr. Solomon's rich aunt in Cheltenham, or Mr. Soloman's rich creditor in Berlin. The elaborate machinery which was once used to make men responsible is now used solely in order to shift the responsibility. People talk about the pride of tyrants; but we in this age are not suffering from the pride of tyrants. We are suffering from the shyness of tyrants; from the shrinking modesty of tyrants. Therefore we must not encourage leader-writers to be shy; we must not inflame their already exaggerated modesty. Rather we must attempt to lure them to be vain and ostentatious; so that through ostentation they may at last find their way to honesty.

The last indictment against this book is the worst of all. It is simply this: that if all goes well this book will be unintelligible gibberish. For it is mostly concerned with attacking attitudes which are in their nature accidental and incapable of enduring. Brief as is the career of such a book as this, it may last just twenty minutes longer than most of the philosophies that it attacks. In the end it will not matter to us whether we wrote well or ill; whether we fought with flails or reeds. It will matter to us greatly on what side we fought.

COCKNEYS AND THEIR JOKES

A writer in the *Yorkshire Evening Post* is very angry indeed with my performances in this column. His precise terms of reproach are, "Mr. G. K. Chesterton is not a humourist: not even a Cockney humourist." I do not mind his saying that I am not a humourist—in which (to tell the truth) I think he is quite right. But I do resent his saying that I am not a Cockney. That envenomed arrow, I admit, went home. If a French writer said of me, "He is no metaphysician: not even an English metaphysician," I could swallow the insult to my metaphysics, but I should feel angry about the insult to my country. So I do not urge that I am a humourist; but I do insist that I am a Cockney. If I were a humourist, I should certainly be a Cockney humourist; if I were a saint, I should certainly be a Cockney saint. I need not recite the splendid catalogue of Cockney saints who have written their names on our noble old City churches. I need not trouble you with the long list of the Cockney humourists who have discharged their bills (or failed to discharge them) in our noble old City taverns. We can weep together over the pathos of the poor Yorkshireman, whose county has never produced some humour not intelligible to the rest of the world. And we can smile together when he says that somebody or other is "not even" a Cockney humourist like Samuel Johnson or Charles Lamb. It is surely sufficiently obvious that all the best humour that exists in our language is Cockney humour. Chaucer was a Cockney; he had his house close to the Abbey. Dickens was a Cockney; he said he could not think without the London streets. The London taverns heard always the quaintest conversation, whether it was Ben Johnson's at the Mermaid or Sam Johnson's at the Cock. Even in our own time it may be noted that the most vital and genuine humour is still written about London. Of this type is the mild and humane irony which marks Mr. Pett Ridge's studies of the small grey streets. Of this type is the simple but smashing laughter of the best tales of Mr. W. W. Jacobs, telling of the smoke and sparkle of the Thames. No; I concede that I am not a Cockney humourist. No; I am not worthy to be. Some time, after sad and strenuous after-lives; some time, after fierce and apocalyptic incarnations; in some strange world beyond the stars, I may become at last a Cockney humourist. In that potential paradise I may walk among the Cockney humourists, if not an equal, at least a companion. I may feel for a moment on my shoulder the hearty hand of Dryden and thread the labyrinths of the sweet insanity of Lamb. But that could only be if I were not only much cleverer, but much better than I am. Before I reach that sphere I shall have left behind, perhaps, the sphere that is inhabited by angels, and even passed that which is appropriated exclusively to the use of Yorkshiremen.

No; London is in this matter attacked upon its strongest ground. London is the largest of the bloated modern cities; London is the smokiest; London is the dirtiest; London is, if you will, the most sombre; London is, if you will, the most miserable. But London is certainly the most amusing and the most amused. You may prove that we have the most tragedy; the fact remains that we have the most comedy, that we have the most farce. We have at the very worst a splendid hypocrisy of humour. We conceal our sorrow behind a screaming derision. You speak of people who laugh through their tears; it is our boast that we only weep through our laughter. There remains always this great boast, perhaps the greatest boast that is possible to human nature. I mean the great boast that the most unhappy part of our population is also the most hilarious part. The poor can forget that social problem which we (the moderately rich) ought never to forget. Blessed are the poor; for they alone have not the poor always with them. The honest poor can sometimes forget poverty. The honest rich can never forget it.

I believe firmly in the value of all vulgar notions, especially of vulgar jokes. When once you have got hold of a vulgar joke, you may be certain that you have got hold of a subtle and spiritual idea. The men who made the joke saw something deep which they could not express except by something silly and emphatic. They saw something delicate which they could only express by something indelicate. I remember that Mr. Max Beerbohm (who has every merit except democracy) attempted to analyse the jokes at which the mob laughs. He divided them into three sections: jokes about bodily humiliation, jokes about things alien, such as foreigners, and jokes about bad cheese. Mr. Max Beerbohm thought he understood the first two forms; but I am not sure that he did. In order to understand vulgar humour it is not enough to be humorous. One must also be vulgar, as I am. And in the first case it is surely obvious that it is not merely at the fact of something being hurt that we laugh (as I trust we do) when a Prime Minister sits down on his hat. If that were so we should laugh whenever we saw a funeral. We do not laugh at the mere fact of something falling down; there is nothing humorous about leaves falling or the sun going down. When our house falls down we do not laugh. All the birds of the air might drop around us in a perpetual shower like a hailstorm without arousing a smile. If you really ask yourself why we laugh at a man sitting down suddenly in the street you will discover that the reason is not only recondite, but ultimately religious. All the jokes about men sitting down on their hats are really theological jokes; they are concerned with the Dual Nature of Man. They refer to the primary paradox that man is superior to all the things around him and yet is at their mercy.

Quite equally subtle and spiritual is the idea at the back of laughing at foreigners. It concerns the almost torturing truth of a thing being like oneself and yet not like oneself. Nobody laughs at what is entirely foreign; nobody laughs at a palm tree. But it is funny to see the familiar image of God disguised behind the black beard of a Frenchman or the black face of a Negro. There is nothing funny in the sounds that are wholly inhuman, the howling of wild beasts or of the wind. But if a man begins to talk like oneself, but all the syllables come out different, then if one is a man one feels inclined to laugh, though if one is a gentleman one resists the inclination.

Mr. Max Beerbohm, I remember, professed to understand the first two forms of popular wit, but said that the third quite stumped him. He could not see why there should be anything funny about bad cheese. I can tell him at once. He has missed the idea because it is subtle and philosophical, and he was looking for something ignorant and foolish. Bad cheese is funny because it is (like the foreigner or the man fallen on the pavement) the type of the transition or transgression across a great mystical boundary. Bad cheese symbolises the change from the inorganic to the organic. Bad cheese symbolises the startling prodigy of matter taking on vitality. It symbolises the origin of life itself. And it is only about such solemn matters as the origin of life that the democracy condescends to joke. Thus, for instance, the democracy jokes about marriage, because marriage is a part of mankind. But the democracy would never deign to joke about Free Love, because Free Love is a piece of priggishness.

As a matter of fact, it will be generally found that the popular joke is not true to the letter, but is true to the spirit. The vulgar joke is generally in the oddest way the truth and yet not the fact. For instance, it is not in the least true that mothers-in-law are as a class oppressive and intolerable; most of them are both devoted and useful. All the mothers-in-law I have ever had were admirable. Yet the legend of the comic papers is profoundly true. It draws attention to the fact that it is much harder to be a nice mother-in-law than to be nice in any other conceivable relation of life. The caricatures have drawn the worst mother-in-law a monster, by way of expressing the fact that the best mother-in-law is a problem. The same is true of the perpetual jokes in comic papers about shrewish wives and henpecked husbands. It is all a frantic exaggeration, but it is an exaggeration of a truth; whereas all the modern mouthings about oppressed women are the exaggerations of a falsehood. If you read even the best of the intellectuals of to-day you will find them saying that in the mass of the democracy the woman is the chattel of her lord, like his bath or his bed. But if you read the comic literature of the democracy you will find that the lord hides under the bed to escape from the wrath of his chattel. This is not the fact, but it is much nearer the truth. Every man who is married knows quite well, not only that he does not regard his wife as a chattel, but that no man can conceivably ever have done so. The joke stands for an ultimate truth, and that is a subtle truth. It is one not very easy to state correctly. It can, perhaps, be most correctly stated by saying that, even if the man is the head of the house, he knows he is the figurehead.

But the vulgar comic papers are so subtle and true that they are even prophetic. If you really want to know what is going to happen to the future of our democracy, do not read the modern sociological prophecies, do not read even Mr. Wells's Utopias for this purpose, though you should certainly read them if you are fond of good honesty and good English. If you want to know what will happen, study the pages of *Snaps* or *Patchy Bits* as if they were the dark tablets graven with the oracles of the gods. For, mean and gross as they are, in all seriousness, they contain what is entirely absent from all Utopias and all the sociological conjectures of our time: they contain some hint of the actual habits and manifest desires of the English people. If we are really to find out what the democracy will ultimately do with itself, we shall surely find it, not in the literature which studies the people, but in the literature which the people studies.

I can give two chance cases in which the common or Cockney joke was a much better prophecy than the careful observations of the most cultured observer. When England was agitated, previous to the last General Election, about the existence of Chinese labour, there was a distinct difference between the tone of the politicians and the tone of the populace. The politicians who disapproved of Chinese labour were most careful to explain that they did not in any sense disapprove of Chinese. According to them, it was a pure question of legal propriety, of whether certain clauses in the contract of indenture were not inconsistent with our constitutional traditions: according to them, the case would have been the same if the people had been Kaffirs or Englishmen. It all sounded wonderfully enlightened and lucid; and in comparison the popular joke looked, of course, very poor. For the popular joke against the Chinese labourers was simply that they were Chinese; it was an objection to an alien type; the popular papers were full of gibes about pigtails and yellow faces. It seemed that the Liberal politicians were raising an intellectual objection to a doubtful document of State; while it seemed that the Radical populace were merely roaring with idiotic laughter at the sight of a Chinaman's clothes. But the popular instinct was justified, for the vices revealed were Chinese vices.

But there is another case more pleasant and more up to date. The popular papers always persisted in representing the New Woman or the Suffragette as an ugly woman, fat, in spectacles, with bulging clothes, and generally falling off a bicycle. As a matter of plain external fact, there was not a word of truth in this. The leaders of the movement of female emancipation are not at all ugly; most of them are extraordinarily good-looking. Nor are they at all indifferent to art or decorative costume; many of them are alarmingly attached to these things. Yet the popular instinct was right. For the popular instinct was that in this movement, rightly or wrongly, there was an element of indifference to female dignity, of a quite new willingness of women to be grotesque. These women did truly despise the pontifical quality of woman. And in our streets and around our Parliament we have seen the stately woman of art and culture turn into the comic woman of *Comic Bits*. And whether we think the exhibition justifiable or not, the prophecy of the comic papers is justified: the healthy and vulgar masses were conscious of a hidden enemy to their traditions who has now come out into the daylight, that the scriptures might be fulfilled. For the two things that a healthy person hates most between heaven and hell are a woman who is not dignified and a man who is.

THE FALLACY OF SUCCESS

There has appeared in our time a particular class of books and articles which I sincerely and solemnly think may be called the silliest ever known among men. They are much more wild than the wildest romances of chivalry and much more dull than the dullest religious tract. Moreover, the romances of chivalry were at least about chivalry; the religious tracts are about religion. But these things are about nothing; they are about what is called Success. On every bookstall, in every magazine, you may find works telling people how to succeed. They are books showing men how to succeed in everything; they are written by men who cannot even succeed in writing books. To begin with, of course, there is no such thing as Success. Or, if you like to put it so, there is nothing that is not successful. That a thing is successful merely means that it is; a millionaire is successful in being a millionaire and a donkey in being a donkey. Any live man has succeeded in living; any dead man may have succeeded in committing suicide. But, passing over the bad logic and bad philosophy in the phrase, we may take it, as these writers do, in the ordinary sense of success in obtaining money or worldly position. These writers profess to tell the ordinary man how he may succeed in his trade or speculation—how, if he is a builder, he may succeed as a builder; how, if he is a stockbroker, he may succeed as a stockbroker. They profess to show him how, if he is a grocer, he may become a sporting yachtsman; how, if he is a tenth-rate journalist, he may become a peer; and how, if he is a German Jew, he may become an Anglo-Saxon. This is a definite and business-like proposal, and I really think that the people who buy these books (if any people do buy them) have a moral, if not a legal, right to ask for their money back. Nobody would dare to publish a book about electricity which literally told one nothing about electricity; no one would dare to publish an article on botany which showed that the writer did not know which end of a plant grew in the earth. Yet our modern world is full of books about Success and successful people which literally contain no kind of idea, and scarcely any kind of verbal sense.

It is perfectly obvious that in any decent occupation (such as bricklaying or writing books) there are only two ways (in any special sense) of succeeding. One is by doing very good work, the other is by cheating. Both are much too simple to require any literary explanation. If you are in for the high jump, either jump higher than any one else, or manage somehow to pretend that you have done so. If you want to succeed at whist, either be a good whist-player, or play with marked cards. You may want a book about jumping; you may want a book about whist; you may want a book about cheating at whist. But you cannot want a book about Success. Especially you cannot want a book about Success such as those which you can now find scattered by the hundred about the book-market. You

5

may want to jump or to play cards; but you do not want to read wandering statements to the effect that jumping is jumping, or that games are won by winners. If these writers, for instance, said anything about success in jumping it would be something like this: "The jumper must have a clear aim before him. He must desire definitely to jump higher than the other men who are in for the same competition. He must let no feeble feelings of mercy (sneaked from the sickening Little Englanders and Pro-Boers) prevent him from trying to *do his best*. He must remember that a competition in jumping is distinctly competitive, and that, as Darwin has gloriously demonstrated, THE WEAKEST GO TO THE WALL." That is the kind of thing the book would say, and very useful it would be, no doubt, if read out in a low and tense voice to a young man just about to take the high jump. Or suppose that in the course of his intellectual rambles the philosopher of Success dropped upon our other case, that of playing cards, his bracing advice would run—"In playing cards it is very necessary to avoid the mistake (commonly made by maudlin humanitarians and Free Traders) of permitting your opponent to win the game. You must have grit and snap and go *in to win*. The days of idealism and superstition are over. We live in a time of science and hard common sense, and it has now been definitely proved that in any game where two are playing IF ONE DOES NOT WIN THE OTHER WILL." It is all very stirring, of course; but I confess that if I were playing cards I would rather have some decent little book which told me the rules of the game. Beyond the rules of the game it is all a question either of talent or dishonesty; and I will undertake to provide either one or the other—which, it is not for me to say.

Turning over a popular magazine, I find a queer and amusing example. There is an article called "The Instinct that Makes People Rich." It is decorated in front with a formidable portrait of Lord Rothschild. There are many definite methods, honest and dishonest, which make people rich; the only "instinct" I know of which does it is that instinct which theological Christianity crudely describes as "the sin of avarice." That, however, is beside the present point. I wish to quote the following exquisite paragraphs as a piece of typical advice as to how to succeed. It is so practical; it leaves so little doubt about what should be our next step—

"The name of Vanderbilt is synonymous with wealth gained by modern enterprise. 'Cornelius,' the founder of the family, was the first of the great American magnates of commerce. He started as the son of a poor farmer; he ended as a millionaire twenty times over.

"He had the money-making instinct. He seized his opportunities, the opportunities that were given by the application of the steam-engine to ocean traffic, and by the birth of railway locomotion in the wealthy but undeveloped United States of America, and consequently he amassed an immense fortune.

"Now it is, of course, obvious that we cannot all follow exactly in the footsteps of this great railway monarch. The precise opportunities that fell to him do not occur to us. Circumstances have changed. But, although this is so, still, in our own sphere and in our own circumstances, we *can* follow his general methods; we can seize those opportunities that are given us, and give ourselves a very fair chance of attaining riches."

In such strange utterances we see quite clearly what is really at the bottom of all these articles and books. It is not mere business; it is not even mere cynicism. It is mysticism; the horrible mysticism of money. The writer of that passage did not really have the remotest notion of how Vanderbilt made his money, or of how anybody else is to make his. He does, indeed, conclude his remarks by advocating some scheme; but it has nothing in the world to do with Vanderbilt. He merely wished to prostrate himself before the mystery of a millionaire. For when we really worship anything, we love not only its clearness but its obscurity. We exult in its very invisibility. Thus, for instance, when a man is in love with a woman he takes special pleasure in the fact that a woman is unreasonable. Thus, again, the very pious poet, celebrating his Creator, takes pleasure in saying that God moves in a mysterious way. Now, the writer of the paragraph which I have quoted does not seem to have had anything to do with a god, and I should not think (judging by his extreme unpracticality) that he had ever been really in love with a woman. But the thing he does worship—Vanderbilt—he treats in exactly this mystical manner. He really revels in the fact his deity Vanderbilt is keeping a secret from him. And it fills his soul with a sort of transport of cunning, an ecstasy of priestcraft, that he should pretend to be telling to the multitude that terrible secret which he does not know.

Speaking about the instinct that makes people rich, the same writer remarks—

"In olden days its existence was fully understood. The Greeks enshrined it in the story of Midas, of the 'Golden Touch.' Here was a man who turned everything he laid his hands upon into gold. His life was a progress amidst riches. Out of everything that came in his way he created the precious metal. 'A foolish legend,' said the wiseacres of the Victorian age. 'A truth,' say we of to-day. We all know of such men. We are ever meeting or reading about such persons who turn everything they touch into gold. Success dogs their very footsteps. Their life's pathway leads unerringly upwards. They cannot fail."

Unfortunately, however, Midas could fail; he did. His path did not lead unerringly upward. He starved because whenever he touched a biscuit or a ham sandwich it turned to gold. That was the whole point of the story, though the writer has to suppress it delicately, writing so near to a portrait of Lord Rothschild. The old fables of mankind are, indeed, unfathomably wise; but we must not have them expurgated in the interests of Mr. Vanderbilt. We must not have King Midas represented as an example of success; he was a failure of an unusually painful kind. Also, he had the ears of an ass. Also (like most other prominent and wealthy persons) he endeavoured to conceal the fact. It was his barber (if I remember right) who had to be treated on a confidential footing with regard to this peculiarity; and his barber, instead of behaving like a go-ahead person of the Succeed-at-all-costs school and trying to blackmail King Midas, went away and whispered this splendid piece of society scandal to the reeds, who enjoyed it enormously. It is said that they also whispered it as the winds swayed them to and fro. I look reverently at the portrait of Lord Rothschild; I read reverently about the exploits of Mr. Vanderbilt. I know that I cannot turn everything I touch to gold; but then I also know that I have never tried, having a preference for other substances, such as grass, and good wine. I know that these people have certainly succeeded in something; that they have certainly overcome somebody; I know that they are kings in a sense that no men were ever kings before; that they create markets and bestride continents. Yet it always seems to me that there is some small domestic fact that they are hiding, and I have sometimes thought I heard upon the wind the laughter and whisper of the reeds.

At least, let us hope that we shall all live to see these absurd books about Success covered with a proper derision and neglect. They do not teach people to be successful, but they do teach people to be snobbish; they do spread a sort of evil poetry of worldliness. The Puritans are always denouncing books that inflame lust; what shall we say of books that inflame the viler passions of avarice and pride? A hundred years ago we had the ideal of the Industrious Apprentice; boys were told that by thrift and work they would all become Lord Mayors. This was fallacious, but it was manly, and had a minimum of moral truth. In our society, temperance will not help a poor man to enrich himself, but it may help him to respect himself. Good work will not make him a rich man, but good work may make him a good workman. The Industrious Apprentice rose by virtues few and narrow indeed, but still virtues. But what shall we say of the gospel preached to the new Industrious Apprentice; the Apprentice who rises not by his virtues, but avowedly by his vices?

ON RUNNING AFTER ONE'S HAT

I feel an almost savage envy on hearing that London has been flooded in my absence, while I am in the mere country. My own Battersea has been, I understand, particularly favoured as a meeting of the waters. Battersea was already, as I need hardly say, the most beautiful of human localities. Now that it has the additional splendour of great sheets of water, there must be something quite incomparable in the landscape (or waterscape) of my own romantic town. Battersea must be a vision of Venice. The boat that brought the meat from the butcher's must have shot along those lanes of rippling silver with the strange smoothness of the gondola. The greengrocer who brought cabbages to the corner of the Latchmere Road must have leant upon the oar with the unearthly grace of the gondolier. There is nothing so perfectly poetical as an island; and when a district is flooded it becomes an archipelago.

Some consider such romantic views of flood or fire slightly lacking in reality. But really this romantic view of such inconveniences is quite as practical as the other. The true optimist who sees in such things an opportunity for enjoyment is quite as logical and much more sensible than the ordinary "Indignant Ratepayer" who sees in them an opportunity for grumbling. Real pain, as in the case of being burnt at Smithfield or having a toothache, is a positive thing; it can be supported, but scarcely enjoyed. But, after all, our toothaches are the exception, and as for being burnt at Smithfield, it only happens to us at the very longest intervals. And most of the inconveniences that make men swear or women cry are really sentimental or imaginative inconveniences—things altogether of the mind. For instance, we often hear grown-up people complaining of having to hang about a railway station and wait for a train. Did you ever hear a small boy complain of having to hang about a railway station and wait for a train? No; for to him to be inside a railway station is to be inside a cavern of wonder and a palace of poetical pleasures. Because to him the red light and the green light on the signal are like a new sun and a new moon. Because to him when the wooden arm of the signal falls down suddenly, it is as if a great king had thrown down his staff as a signal and started a shrieking tournament of trains. I myself am of little boys' habit in this matter. They also serve who only stand and wait for the two fifteen. Their meditations may be full of rich and fruitful things. Many of the most purple hours of my life have been passed at Clapham Junction, which is now, I suppose, under water. I have been there in many moods so fixed and mystical that the water might well have come up to my waist before I noticed it particularly. But in the case of all such annoyances, as I have said, everything depends upon the emotional point of view. You can safely apply the test to almost every one of the things that are currently talked of as the typical nuisance of daily life.

For instance, there is a current impression that it is unpleasant to have to run after one's hat. Why should it be unpleasant to the well-ordered and pious mind? Not merely because it is running, and running exhausts one. The same people run much faster in games and sports. The same people run much more eagerly after an uninteresting; little leather ball than they will after a nice silk hat. There is an idea that it is humiliating to run after one's hat; and when people say it is humiliating they mean that it is comic. It certainly is comic; but man is a very comic creature, and most of the things he does are comic—eating, for instance. And the most comic things of all are exactly the things that are most worth doing—such as making love. A man running after a hat is not half so ridiculous as a man running after a wife.

Now a man could, if he felt rightly in the matter, run after his hat with the manliest ardour and the most sacred joy. He might regard himself as a jolly huntsman pursuing a wild animal, for certainly no animal could be wilder. In fact, I am inclined to believe that hat-hunting on windy days will be the sport of the upper classes in the future. There will be a meet of ladies and gentlemen on some high ground on a gusty morning. They will be told that the professional attendants have started a hat in such-and-such a thicket, or whatever be the technical term. Notice that this employment will in the fullest degree combine sport with humanitarianism. The hunters would feel that they were not inflicting pain. Nay, they would feel that they were inflicting pleasure, rich, almost riotous pleasure, upon the people who were looking on. When last I saw an old gentleman running after his hat in Hyde Park, I told him that a heart so benevolent as his ought to be filled with peace and thanks at the thought of how much unaffected pleasure his every gesture and bodily attitude were at that moment giving to the crowd.

The same principle can be applied to every other typical domestic worry. A gentleman trying to get a fly out of the milk or a piece of cork out of his glass of wine often imagines himself to be irritated. Let him think for a moment of the patience of anglers sitting by dark pools, and let his soul be immediately irradiated with gratification and repose. Again, I have known some people of very modern views driven by their distress to the use of theological terms to which they attached no doctrinal significance, merely because a drawer was jammed tight and they could not pull it out. A friend of mine was particularly afflicted in this way. Every day his drawer was jammed, and every day in consequence it was something else that rhymes to it. But I pointed out to him that this sense of wrong was really subjective and relative; it rested entirely upon the assumption that the drawer could, should, and would come out easily. "But if," I said, "you picture to yourself that you are pulling against some powerful and oppressive enemy, the struggle will become merely exciting and not exasperating. Imagine that you are tugging up a lifeboat out of the sea. Imagine that you are roping up a fellow-creature out of an Alpine crevass. Imagine even that you are a boy again and engaged in a tug-of-war between French and English." Shortly after saying this I left him; but I have no doubt at all that my words bore the best possible fruit. I have no doubt that every day of his life he hangs on to the handle of that drawer with a flushed face and eyes bright with battle, uttering encouraging shouts to himself, and seeming to hear all round him the roar of an applauding ring.

So I do not think that it is altogether fanciful or incredible to suppose that even the floods in London may be accepted and enjoyed poetically. Nothing beyond inconvenience seems really to have been caused by them; and inconvenience, as I have said, is only one aspect, and that the most unimaginative and accidental aspect of a really romantic situation. An adventure is only an inconvenience rightly considered. An inconvenience is only an adventure wrongly considered. The water that girdled the houses and shops of London must, if anything, have only increased their previous witchery and wonder. For as the Roman Catholic priest in the story said: "Wine is good with everything except water," and on a similar principle, water is good with everything except wine.

THE VOTE AND THE HOUSE

Most of us will be canvassed soon, I suppose; some of us may even canvass. Upon which side, of course, nothing will induce me to state, beyond saying that by a remarkable coincidence it will in every case be the only side in which a high-minded, public-spirited, and patriotic citizen can take even a momentary interest. But the general question of canvassing itself, being a non-party question, is one which we may be permitted to approach. The rules for canvassers are fairly familiar to any one who has ever canvassed. They are printed on the little card which you carry about with you and lose. There is a statement, I think, that you must not offer a voter food or drink. However hospitable you may feel towards him in his own house, you must not carry his lunch about with you. You must not produce a veal cutlet from your tail-coat pocket. You must not conceal poached eggs about your person. You must not, like a kind of conjurer, produce baked potatoes from your hat. In short, the canvasser must not feed the voter in any way. Whether the voter is allowed to feed the canvasser, whether the voter may give the canvasser veal cutlets and baked potatoes, is a point of law on which I have never been able to inform myself. When I found myself canvassing a gentleman, I have sometimes felt tempted to ask him if there was any rule against his giving me food and drink; but the matter seemed a delicate one to approach. His attitude to me also sometimes suggested a doubt as to whether he would, even if he could. But there are voters who might find it worth while to discover if there is any law against bribing a canvasser. They might bribe him to go away.

The second veto for canvassers which was printed on the little card said that you must not persuade any one to personate a voter. I have no idea what it means. To dress up as an average voter seems a little vague. There is no well-recognised uniform, as far as I know, with civic waistcoat and patriotic whiskers. The enterprise resolves itself into one somewhat similar to the enterprise of a rich friend of mine who went to a fancy-dress ball dressed up as a gentleman. Perhaps it means that there is a practice of personating some individual voter. The canvasser creeps to the house of his fellow-conspirator carrying a make-up in a bag. He produces from it a pair of white moustaches and a single eyeglass, which are sufficient to give the most common-place person a startling resemblance to the Colonel at No. 80. Or he hurriedly affixes to his friend that large nose and that bald head which are all that is essential to an illusion of the presence of Professor Budger. I do not undertake to unravel these knots. I can only say that when I was a canvasser I was told by the little card, with every circumstance of seriousness and authority, that I was not to persuade anybody to personate a voter: and I can lay my hand upon my heart and affirm that I never did.

The third injunction on the card was one which seemed to me, if interpreted exactly and according to its words, to undermine the very foundations of our politics. It told me that I must not "threaten a voter with any consequence whatever." No doubt this was intended to apply to threats of a personal and illegitimate character; as, for instance, if a wealthy candidate were to threaten to raise all the rents, or to put up a statue of himself. But as verbally and grammatically expressed, it certainly would cover those general threats of disaster to the whole community which are the main matter of political discussion. When a canvasser says that if the opposition candidate gets in the country will be ruined, he is threatening the voters with certain consequences. When the Free Trader says that if Tariffs are adopted the people in Brompton or Bayswater will crawl about eating grass, he is threatening them with consequences. When the Tariff Reformer says that if Free Trade exists for another year St. Paul's Cathedral will be a ruin and Ludgate Hill as deserted as Stonehenge, he is also threatening. And what is the good of being a Tariff Reformer if you can't say that? What is the use of being a politician or a Parliamentary candidate at all if one cannot tell the people that if the other man gets in, England will be instantly invaded and enslaved, blood be pouring down the Strand, and all the English ladies carried off into harems. But these things are, after all, consequences, so to speak.

The majority of refined persons in our day may generally be heard abusing the practice of canvassing. In the same way the majority of refined persons (commonly the same refined persons) may be heard abusing the practice of interviewing celebrities. It seems a very singular thing to me that this refined world reserves all its indignation for the comparatively open and innocent element in both walks of life. There is really a vast amount of corruption and hypocrisy in our election politics; about the most honest thing in the whole mess is the canvassing. A man has not got a right to "nurse" a constituency with aggressive charities, to buy it with great presents of parks and libraries, to open vague vistas of future benevolence; all this, which goes on unrebuked, is bribery and nothing else. But a man has got the right to go to another free man and ask him with civility whether he will vote for him. The information can be asked, granted, or refused without any loss of dignity on either side, which is more than can be said of a park. It is the same with the place of interviewing in journalism. In a trade where there are labyrinths of insincerity, interviewing is about the most simple and the most sincere thing there is. The canvasser, when he wants to know a man's opinions, goes and asks him. It may be a bore; but it is about as plain and straight a thing as he could do. So the interviewer, when he wants to know a man's opinions, goes and asks him. Again, it may be a bore; but again, it is about as plain and straight as anything could be. But all the other real and systematic cynicisms of our journalism pass without being vituperated and even without being known—the financial motives of policy, the misleading posters, the suppression of just letters of complaint. A statement about a man may be infamously untrue, but it is read calmly. But a statement by a man to an interviewer is felt as indefensibly vulgar. That the paper should misrepresent him is nothing; that he should represent himself is bad taste. The whole error in both cases lies in the fact that the refined persons are attacking politics and journalism on the ground of vulgarity. Of course, politics and journalism are, as it happens, very vulgar. But their vulgarity is not the worst thing about them. Things are so bad with both that by this time their vulgarity is the best thing about them. Their vulgarity is at least a noisy thing; and their great danger is that silence that always comes before decay. The conversational persuasion at elections is perfectly human and rational; it is the silent persuasions that are utterly damnable.

If it is true that the Commons' House will not hold all the Commons, it is a very good example of what we call the anomalies of the English Constitution. It is also, I think, a very good example of how highly undesirable those anomalies really are. Most Englishmen say that these anomalies do not matter; they are not ashamed of being illogical; they are proud of being illogical. Lord Macaulay (a very typical Englishman, romantic, prejudiced, poetical), Lord Macaulay said that he would not lift his hand to get rid of an anomaly that was not also a grievance. Many other sturdy romantic Englishmen say the same. They boast of our anomalies; they boast of our illogicality; they say it shows what a practical people we are. They are utterly wrong. Lord Macaulay was in this matter, as in a few others, utterly wrong. Anomalies do matter very much, and do a great deal of harm; abstract illogicalities do matter a great deal, and do a great deal of harm. And this for a reason that any one at all acquainted with human nature can see for himself. All injustice begins in the mind. And anomalies accustom the mind to the idea of unreason and untruth. Suppose I had by some prehistoric law the power of forcing every man in Battersea to nod his head three times before he got out of bed. The practical politicians might say that this power was a harmless anomaly; that it was not a grievance. It could do my subjects no harm; it could do me no good. The people of Battersea, they would say, might safely submit to it. But the people of Battersea could not safely submit to it, for all that. If I had nodded their heads for them for fifty years I could cut off their heads for them at the end of it with immeasurably greater ease. For there would have permanently sunk into every man's mind the notion that it was a natural thing for me to have a fantastic and irrational power. They would have grown accustomed to insanity.

For, in order that men should resist injustice, something more is necessary than that they should think injustice unpleasant. They must think injustice *absurd*; above all, they must think it startling. They must retain the violence of a virgin astonishment. That is the explanation of the singular fact which must have struck many people in the relations of philosophy and reform. It is the fact (I mean) that optimists are more practical reformers than pessimists. Superficially, one would imagine that the railer would be the reformer; that the man who thought that everything was wrong would be the man to put everything right. In historical practice the thing is quite the other way; curiously enough, it is the man who likes things as they are who really makes them better. The optimist Dickens has achieved more reforms than the pessimist Gissing. A man like Rousseau has far too rosy a theory of human nature; but he produces a revolution. A man like David Hume thinks that almost all things are depressing; but he is a Conservative, and wishes to keep them as they are. A man like Godwin believes existence to be kindly; but he is a rebel. A man like Carlyle believes existence to be cruel; but he is a Tory. Everywhere the man who alters things begins by liking things. And the real explanation of this success of the optimistic reformer, of this failure of the pessimistic reformer, is, after all, an explanation of sufficient simplicity. It is because the optimist can look at wrong not only with indignation, but with a startled indignation. When the pessimist looks at any infamy, it is to him, after all, only a repetition of the infamy of existence. The Court of Chancery is indefensible—like mankind. The Inquisition is abominable—like the universe. But the optimist sees injustice as something discordant and unexpected, and it stings him into action. The pessimist can be enraged at wrong; but only the optimist can be surprised at it.

And it is the same with the relations of an anomaly to the logical mind. The pessimist resents evil (like Lord Macaulay) solely because it is a grievance. The optimist resents it also, because it is an anomaly; a contradiction to his conception of the course of things. And it is not at all unimportant, but on the contrary most important, that this course of things in politics and elsewhere should be lucid, explicable and defensible. When people have got used to unreason they can no longer be startled at injustice. When people have grown familiar with an anomaly, they are prepared to that extent for a grievance; they may think the grievance grievous, but they can no longer think it strange. Take, if only as an excellent example, the very matter alluded to before; I mean the seats, or rather the lack of seats, in the House of Commons. Perhaps it is true that under the best conditions it would never happen that every member turned up. Perhaps a complete attendance would never actually be. But who can tell how much influence in keeping members away may have been exerted by this calm assumption that they would stop away? How can any man be expected to help to make a full attendance when he knows that a full attendance is actually forbidden? How can the men who make up the Chamber do their duty reasonably when the very men who built the House have not done theirs reasonably? If the trumpet give an uncertain sound, who shall prepare himself for the battle? And what if the remarks of the trumpet take this form, "I charge you as you love your King and country to come to this Council. And I know you won't."

CONCEIT AND CARICATURE

If a man must needs be conceited, it is certainly better that he should be conceited about some merits or talents that he does not really possess. For then his vanity remains more or less superficial; it remains a mere mistake of fact, like that of a man who thinks he inherits the royal blood or thinks he has an infallible system for Monte Carlo. Because the merit is an unreal merit, it does not corrupt or sophisticate his real merits. He is vain about the virtue he has not got; but he may be humble about the virtues that he has got. His truly honourable qualities remain in their primordial innocence; he cannot see them and he cannot spoil them. If a man's mind is erroneously possessed with the idea that he is a great violinist, that need not prevent his being a gentleman and an honest man. But if once his mind is possessed in any strong degree with the knowledge that he is a gentleman, he will soon cease to be one.

But there is a third kind of satisfaction of which I have noticed one or two examples lately—

another kind of satisfaction which is neither a pleasure in the virtues that we do possess nor a pleasure in the virtues we do not possess. It is the pleasure which a man takes in the presence or absence of certain things in himself without ever adequately asking himself whether in his case they constitute virtues at all. A man will plume himself because he is not bad in some particular way, when the truth is that he is not good enough to be bad in that particular way. Some priggish little clerk will say, "I have reason to congratulate myself that I am a civilised person, and not so bloodthirsty as the Mad Mullah." Somebody ought to say to him, "A really good man would be less bloodthirsty than the Mullah. But you are less bloodthirsty, not because you are more of a good man, but because you are a great deal less of a man. You are not bloodthirsty, not because you would spare your enemy, but because you would run away from him." Or again, some Puritan with a sullen type of piety would say, "I have reason to congratulate myself that I do not worship graven images like the old heathen Greeks." And again somebody ought to say to him, "The best religion may not worship graven images, because it may see beyond them. But if you do not worship graven images, it is only because you are mentally and morally quite incapable of graving them. True religion, perhaps, is above idolatry. But you are below idolatry. You are not holy enough yet to worship a lump of stone."

Mr. F. C. Gould, the brilliant and felicitous caricaturist, recently delivered a most interesting speech upon the nature and atmosphere of our modern English caricature. I think there is really very little to congratulate oneself about in the condition of English caricature. There are few causes for pride; probably the greatest cause for pride is Mr. F. C. Gould. But Mr. F. C. Gould, forbidden by modesty to adduce this excellent ground for optimism, fell back upon saying a thing which is said by numbers of other people, but has not perhaps been said lately with the full authority of an eminent cartoonist. He said that he thought "that they might congratulate themselves that the style of caricature which found acceptation nowadays was very different from the lampoon of the old days." Continuing, he said, according to the newspaper report, "On looking back to the political lampoons of Rowlandson's and Gilray's time they would find them coarse and brutal. In some countries abroad still, 'even in America,' the method of political caricature was of the bludgeon kind. The fact was we had passed the bludgeon stage. If they were brutal in attacking a man, even for political reasons, they roused sympathy for the man who was attacked. What they had to do was to rub in the point they wanted to emphasise as gently as they could." (Laughter and applause.)

Anybody reading these words, and anybody who heard them, will certainly feel that there is in them a great deal of truth, as well as a great deal of geniality. But along with that truth and with that geniality there is a streak of that erroneous type of optimism which is founded on the fallacy of which I have spoken above. Before we congratulate ourselves upon the absence of certain faults from our nation or society, we ought to ask ourselves why it is that these faults are absent. Are we without the fault because we have the opposite virtue? Or are we without the fault because we have the opposite fault? It is a good thing assuredly, to be innocent of any excess; but let us be sure that we are not innocent of excess merely by being guilty of defect. Is it really true that our English political satire is so moderate because it is so magnanimous, so forgiving, so saintly? Is it penetrated through and through with a mystical charity, with a psychological tenderness? Do we spare the feelings of the Cabinet Minister because we pierce through all his apparent crimes and follies down to the dark virtues of which his own soul is unaware? Do we temper the wind to the Leader of the Opposition because in our all-embracing heart we pity and cherish the struggling spirit of the Leader of the Opposition? Briefly, have we left off being brutal because we are too grand and generous to be brutal? Is it really true that we are *better* than brutality? Is it really true that we have *passed* the bludgeon stage?

I fear that there is, to say the least of it, another side to the matter. Is it not only too probable that the mildness of our political satire, when compared with the political satire of our fathers, arises simply from the profound unreality of our current politics? Rowlandson and Gilray did not fight merely because they were naturally pothouse pugilists; they fought because they had something to fight about. It is easy enough to be refined about things that do not matter; but men kicked and plunged a little in that portentous wrestle in which swung to and fro, alike dizzy with danger, the independence of England, the independence of Ireland, the independence of France. If we wish for a proof of this fact that the lack of refinement did not come from mere brutality, the proof is easy. The proof is that in that struggle no personalities were more brutal than the really refined personalities. None were more violent and intolerant than those who were by nature polished and sensitive. Nelson, for instance, had the nerves and good manners of a woman: nobody in his senses, I suppose, would call Nelson "brutal." But when he was touched upon the national matter, there sprang out of him a spout of oaths, and he could only tell men to "Kill! kill! kill the d----d Frenchmen." It would be as easy to take examples on the other side. Camille Desmoulins was a man of much the same type, not only elegant and sweet in temper, but almost tremulously tender and humanitarian. But he was ready, he said, "to embrace Liberty upon a pile of corpses." In Ireland there were even more instances. Robert Emmet was only one famous example of a whole family of men at once sensitive and savage. I think that Mr. F.C. Gould is altogether wrong in talking of this

11

political ferocity as if it were some sort of survival from ruder conditions, like a flint axe or a hairy man. Cruelty is, perhaps, the worst kind of sin. Intellectual cruelty is certainly the worst kind of cruelty. But there is nothing in the least barbaric or ignorant about intellectual cruelty. The great Renaissance artists who mixed colours exquisitely mixed poisons equally exquisitely; the great Renaissance princes who designed instruments of music also designed instruments of torture. Barbarity, malignity, the desire to hurt men, are the evil things generated in atmospheres of intense reality when great nations or great causes are at war. We may, perhaps, be glad that we have not got them: but it is somewhat dangerous to be proud that we have not got them. Perhaps we are hardly great enough to have them. Perhaps some great virtues have to be generated, as in men like Nelson or Emmet, before we can have these vices at all, even as temptations. I, for one, believe that if our caricaturists do not hate their enemies, it is not because they are too big to hate them, but because their enemies are not big enough to hate. I do not think we have passed the bludgeon stage. I believe we have not come to the bludgeon stage. We must be better, braver, and purer men than we are before we come to the bludgeon stage.

Let us then, by all means, be proud of the virtues that we have not got; but let us not be too arrogant about the virtues that we cannot help having. It may be that a man living on a desert island has a right to congratulate himself upon the fact that he can meditate at his ease. But he must not congratulate himself on the fact that he is on a desert island, and at the same time congratulate himself on the self-restraint he shows in not going to a ball every night. Similarly our England may have a right to congratulate itself upon the fact that her politics are very quiet, amicable, and humdrum. But she must not congratulate herself upon that fact and also congratulate herself upon the self-restraint she shows in not tearing herself and her citizens into rags. Between two English Privy Councillors polite language is a mark of civilisation, but really not a mark of magnanimity.

Allied to this question is the kindred question on which we so often hear an innocent British boast—the fact that our statesmen are privately on very friendly relations, although in Parliament they sit on opposite sides of the House. Here, again, it is as well to have no illusions. Our statesmen are not monsters of mystical generosity or insane logic, who are really able to hate a man from three to twelve and to love him from twelve to three. If our social relations are more peaceful than those of France or America or the England of a hundred years ago, it is simply because our politics are more peaceful; not improbably because our politics are more fictitious. If our statesmen agree more in private, it is for the very simple reason that they agree more in public. And the reason they agree so much in both cases is really that they belong to one social class; and therefore the dining life is the real life. Tory and Liberal statesmen like each other, but it is not because they are both expansive; it is because they are both exclusive.

PATRIOTISM AND SPORT.

I notice that some papers, especially papers that call themselves patriotic, have fallen into quite a panic over the fact that we have been twice beaten in the world of sport, that a Frenchman has beaten us at golf, and that Belgians have beaten us at rowing. I suppose that the incidents are important to any people who ever believed in the self-satisfied English legend on this subject. I suppose that there are men who vaguely believe that we could never be beaten by a Frenchman, despite the fact that we have often been beaten by Frenchmen, and once by a Frenchwoman. In the old pictures in *Punch* you will find a recurring piece of satire. The English caricaturists always assumed that a Frenchman could not ride to hounds or enjoy English hunting. It did not seem to occur to them that all the people who founded English hunting were Frenchmen. All the Kings and nobles who originally rode to hounds spoke French. Large numbers of those Englishmen who still ride to hounds have French names. I suppose that the thing is important to any one who is ignorant of such evident matters as these. I suppose that if a man has ever believed that we English have some sacred and separate right to be athletic, such reverses do appear quite enormous and shocking. They feel as if, while the proper sun was rising in the east, some other and unexpected sun had begun to rise in the north-north-west by north. For the benefit, the moral and intellectual benefit of such people, it may be worth while to point out that the Anglo-Saxon has in these cases been defeated precisely by those competitors whom he has always regarded as being out of the running; by Latins, and by Latins of the most easy and unstrenuous type; not only by Frenchman, but by Belgians. All this, I say, is worth telling to any intelligent person who believes in the haughty theory of Anglo-Saxon superiority. But, then, no intelligent person does believe in the haughty theory of Anglo-Saxon superiority. No quite genuine Englishman ever did believe in it. And the genuine Englishman these defeats will in no respect dismay.

The genuine English patriot will know that the strength of England has never depended upon any of these things; that the glory of England has never had anything to do with them, except in the opinion of a large section of the rich and a loose section of the poor which copies the idleness of the rich. These people will, of course, think too much of our failure, just as they thought too much of our success. The typical Jingoes who have admired their countrymen too much for being conquerors will, doubtless, despise their countrymen too much for being conquered. But the Englishman with any feeling for England will know that athletic failures do not prove that England is weak, any more than athletic successes proved that England was strong. The truth is that athletics, like all other things, especially modern, are insanely individualistic. The Englishmen who win sporting prizes are exceptional among Englishmen, for the simple reason that they are exceptional even among men. English athletes represent England just about as much as Mr. Barnum's freaks represent America. There are so few of such people in the whole world that it is almost a toss-up whether they are found in this or that country.

If any one wants a simple proof of this, it is easy to find. When the great English athletes are not exceptional Englishmen they are generally not Englishmen at all. Nay, they are often representatives of races of which the average tone is specially incompatible with athletics. For instance, the English are supposed to rule the natives of India in virtue of their superior hardiness, superior activity, superior health of body and mind. The Hindus are supposed to be our subjects because they are less fond of action, less fond of openness and the open air. In a word, less fond of cricket. And, substantially, this is probably true, that the Indians are less fond of cricket. All the same, if you ask among Englishmen for the very best cricket-player, you will find that he is an Indian. Or, to take another case: it is, broadly speaking, true that the Jews are, as a race, pacific, intellectual, indifferent to war, like the Indians, or, perhaps, contemptuous of war, like the Chinese: nevertheless, of the very good prize-fighters, one or two have been Jews.

This is one of the strongest instances of the particular kind of evil that arises from our English form of the worship of athletics. It concentrates too much upon the success of individuals. It began, quite naturally and rightly, with wanting England to win. The second stage was that it wanted some Englishmen to win. The third stage was (in the ecstasy and agony of some special competition) that it wanted one particular Englishman to win. And the fourth stage was that when he had won, it discovered that he was not even an Englishman.

This is one of the points, I think, on which something might really be said for Lord Roberts and his rather vague ideas which vary between rifle clubs and conscription. Whatever may be the advantages or disadvantages otherwise of the idea, it is at least an idea of procuring equality and a sort of average in the athletic capacity of the people; it might conceivably act as a corrective to our mere tendency to see ourselves in certain exceptional athletes. As it is, there are millions of Englishmen who really think that they are a muscular race because C.B. Fry is an Englishman. And there are many of them who think vaguely that athletics must belong to England because Ranjitsinhji is an Indian.

But the real historic strength of England, physical and moral, has never had anything to do with this athletic specialism; it has been rather hindered by it. Somebody said that the Battle of Waterloo was won on Eton playing-fields. It was a particularly unfortunate remark, for the English contribution to the victory of Waterloo depended very much more than is common in victories upon the steadiness of the rank and file in an almost desperate situation. The Battle of Waterloo was won by the stubbornness of the common soldier—that is to say, it was won by the man who had never been to Eton. It was absurd to say that Waterloo was won on Eton cricket-fields. But it might have been fairly said that Waterloo was won on the village green, where clumsy boys played a very clumsy cricket. In a word, it was the average of the nation that was strong, and athletic glories do not indicate much about the average of a nation. Waterloo was not won by good cricket-players. But Waterloo was won by bad cricket-players, by a mass of men who had some minimum of athletic instincts and habits.

It is a good sign in a nation when such things are done badly. It shows that all the people are doing them. And it is a bad sign in a nation when such things are done very well, for it shows that only a few experts and eccentrics are doing them, and that the nation is merely looking on. Suppose that whenever we heard of walking in England it always meant walking forty-five miles a day without fatigue. We should be perfectly certain that only a few men were walking at all, and that all the other British subjects were being wheeled about in Bath-chairs. But if when we hear of walking it means slow walking, painful walking, and frequent fatigue, then we know that the mass of the nation still is walking. We know that England is still literally on its feet.

The difficulty is therefore that the actual raising of the standard of athletics has probably been bad for national athleticism. Instead of the tournament being a healthy *mêlée* into which any ordinary man would rush and take his chance, it has become a fenced and guarded tilting-yard for the collision of particular champions against whom no ordinary man would pit himself or even be permitted to pit himself. If Waterloo was won on Eton cricket-fields it was because Eton cricket was probably much more careless then than it is now. As long as the game was a game, everybody wanted to join in it. When it becomes an art, every one wants to look at it. When it was frivolous it may have won Waterloo: when it was serious and efficient it lost Magersfontein.

In the Waterloo period there was a general rough-and-tumble athleticism among average Englishmen. It cannot be re-created by cricket, or by conscription, or by any artificial means. It was a thing of the soul. It came out of laughter, religion, and the spirit of the place. But it was like the modern French duel in this—that it might happen to anybody. If I were a French journalist it might really happen that Monsieur Clemenceau might challenge me to meet him with pistols. But I do not think that it is at all likely that Mr. C. B. Fry will ever challenge me to meet him with cricket-bats.

AN ESSAY ON TWO CITIES.

A little while ago I fell out of England into the town of Paris. If a man fell out of the moon into the town of Paris he would know that it was the capital of a great nation. If, however, he fell (perhaps off some other side of the moon) so as to hit the city of London, he would not know so well that it was the capital of a great nation; at any rate, he would not know that the nation was so great as it is. This would be so even on the assumption that the man from the moon could not read our alphabet, as presumably he could not, unless elementary education in that planet has gone to rather unsuspected lengths. But it is true that a great part of the distinctive quality which separates Paris from London may be even seen in the names. Real democrats always insist that England is an aristocratic country. Real aristocrats always insist (for some mysterious reason) that it is a democratic country. But if any one has any real doubt about the matter let him consider simply the names of the streets. Nearly all the streets out of the Strand, for instance, are named after the first name, second name, third name, fourth, fifth, and sixth names of some particular noble family; after their relations, connections, or places of residence—Arundel Street, Norfolk Street, Villiers Street, Bedford Street, Southampton Street, and any number of others. The names are varied, so as to introduce the same family under all sorts of different surnames. Thus we have Arundel Street and also Norfolk Street; thus we have Buckingham Street and also Villiers Street. To say that this is not aristocracy is simply intellectual impudence. I am an ordinary citizen, and my name is Gilbert Keith Chesterton; and I confess that if I found three streets in a row in the Strand, the first called Gilbert Street, the second Keith Street, and the third Chesterton Street, I should consider that I had become a somewhat more important person in the commonwealth than was altogether good for its health. If Frenchmen ran London (which God forbid!), they would think it quite as ludicrous that those streets should be named after the Duke of Buckingham as that they should be named after me. They are streets out of one of the main thoroughfares of London. If French methods were adopted, one of them would be called Shakspere Street, another Cromwell Street, another Wordsworth Street; there would be statues of each of these persons at the end of each of these streets, and any streets left over would be named after the date on which the Reform Bill was passed or the Penny Postage established.

Suppose a man tried to find people in London by the names of the places. It would make a fine farce, illustrating our illogicality. Our hero having once realised that Buckingham Street was named after the Buckingham family, would naturally walk into Buckingham Palace in search of the Duke of Buckingham. To his astonishment he would meet somebody quite different. His simple lunar logic would lead him to suppose that if he wanted the Duke of Marlborough (which seems unlikely) he would find him at Marlborough House. He would find the Prince of Wales. When at last he understood that the Marlboroughs live at Blenheim, named after the great Marlborough's victory, he would, no doubt, go there. But he would again find himself in error if, acting upon this principle, he tried to find the Duke of Wellington, and told the cabman to drive to Waterloo. I wonder that no one has written a wild romance about the adventures of such an alien, seeking the great English aristocrats, and only guided by the names; looking for the Duke of Bedford in the town of that name, seeking for some trace of the Duke of Norfolk in Norfolk. He might sail for Wellington in New Zealand to find the ancient seat of the Wellingtons. The last scene might show him trying to learn Welsh in order to converse with the Prince of Wales.

But even if the imaginary traveller knew no alphabet of this earth at all, I think it would still be possible to suppose him seeing a difference between London and Paris, and, upon the whole, the real difference. He would not be able to read the words "Quai Voltaire;" but he would see the sneering statue and the hard, straight roads; without having heard of Voltaire he would understand that the city was Voltairean. He would not know that Fleet Street was named after the Fleet Prison. But the same national spirit which kept the Fleet Prison closed and narrow still keeps Fleet Street closed and narrow. Or, if you will, you may call Fleet Street cosy, and the Fleet Prison cosy. I think I could be more comfortable in the Fleet Prison, in an English way of comfort, than just under the statue of Voltaire. I think that the man from the moon would know France without knowing French; I think that he would know England without having heard the word. For in the last resort all men talk by signs. To talk by statues is to talk by signs; to talk by cities is to talk by signs. Pillars, palaces, cathedrals, temples, pyramids, are an enormous dumb alphabet: as if some giant held up his fingers of stone. The most important things at the last are always said by signs, even if, like the Cross on St. Paul's, they are signs in heaven. If men do not understand signs, they will never understand words.

For my part, I should be inclined to suggest that the chief object of education should be to restore simplicity. If you like to put it so, the chief object of education is not to learn things; nay, the chief object of education is to unlearn things. The chief object of education is to unlearn all the weariness and wickedness of the world and to get back into that state of exhilaration we all instinctively celebrate when we write by preference of children and of boys. If I were an examiner appointed to examine all examiners (which does not at present appear probable), I would not only ask the teachers how much knowledge they had imparted; I would ask them how much splendid and scornful ignorance they had erected, like some royal tower in arms. But, in any case, I would insist that people should have so much simplicity as would enable them to see things suddenly and to see things as they are. I do not care so much whether they can read the names over the shops. I do care very much whether they can read the shops. I do not feel deeply troubled as to whether they can tell where London is on the map so long as they can tell where Brixton is on the way home. I do not even mind whether they can put two and two together in the mathematical sense; I am content if they can put two and two together in the metaphorical sense. But all this longer statement of an obvious view comes back to the metaphor I have employed. I do not care a dump whether they know the alphabet, so long as they know the dumb alphabet.

Unfortunately, I have noticed in many aspects of our popular education that this is not done at all. One teaches our London children to see London with abrupt and simple eyes. And London is far more difficult to see properly than any other place. London is a riddle. Paris is an explanation. The education of the Parisian child is something corresponding to the clear avenues and the exact squares of Paris. When the Parisian boy has done learning about the French reason and the Roman order he can go out and see the thing repeated in the shapes of many shining public places, in the angles of many streets. But when the English boy goes out, after learning about a vague progress and idealism, he cannot see it anywhere. He cannot see anything anywhere, except Sapolio and the *Daily Mail*. We must either alter London to suit the ideals of our education, or else alter our education to suit the great beauty of London.

FRENCH AND ENGLISH

It is obvious that there is a great deal of difference between being international and being cosmopolitan. All good men are international. Nearly all bad men are cosmopolitan. If we are to be international we must be national. And it is largely because those who call themselves the friends of peace have not dwelt sufficiently on this distinction that they do not impress the bulk of any of the nations to which they belong. International peace means a peace between nations, not a peace after the destruction of nations, like the Buddhist peace after the destruction of personality. The golden age of the good European is like the heaven of the Christian: it is a place where people will love each other; not like the heaven of the Hindu, a place where they will be each other. And in the case of national character this can be seen in a curious way. It will generally be found, I think, that the more a man really appreciates and admires the soul of another people the less he will attempt to imitate it; he will be conscious that there is something in it too deep and too unmanageable to imitate. The Englishman who has a fancy for France will try to be French; the Englishman who admires France will remain obstinately English. This is to be particularly noticed in the case of our relations with the French, because it is one of the outstanding peculiarities of the French that their vices are all on the surface, and their extraordinary virtues concealed. One might almost say that their vices are the flower of their virtues.

Thus their obscenity is the expression of their passionate love of dragging all things into the light. The avarice of their peasants means the independence of their peasants. What the English call their rudeness in the streets is a phase of their social equality. The worried look of their women is connected with the responsibility of their women; and a certain unconscious brutality of hurry and gesture in the men is related to their inexhaustible and extraordinary military courage. Of all countries, therefore, France is the worst country for a superficial fool to admire. Let a fool hate France: if the fool loves it he will soon be a knave. He will certainly admire it, not only for the things that are not creditable, but actually for the things that are not there. He will admire the grace and indolence of the most industrious people in the world. He will admire the romance and fantasy of the most determinedly respectable and commonplace people in the world. This mistake the Englishman will make if he admires France too hastily; but the mistake that he makes about France will be slight compared with the mistake that he makes about himself. An Englishman who professes really to like French realistic novels, really to be at home in a French modern theatre, really to experience no shock on first seeing the savage French caricatures, is making a mistake very dangerous for his own sincerity. He is admiring something he does not understand. He is reaping where he has not sown, and taking up where he has not laid down; he is trying to taste the fruit when he has never toiled over the tree. He is trying to pluck the exquisite fruit of French cynicism, when he has never tilled the rude but rich soil of French virtue.

The thing can only be made clear to Englishmen by turning it round. Suppose a Frenchman came out of democratic France to live in England, where the shadow of the great houses still falls everywhere, and where even freedom was, in its origin, aristocratic. If the Frenchman saw our aristocracy and liked it, if he saw our snobbishness and liked it, if he set himself to imitate it, we all know what we should feel. We all know that we should feel that that particular Frenchman was a repulsive little gnat. He would be imitating English aristocracy; he would be imitating the English vice. But he would not even understand the vice he plagiarised: especially he would not understand that the vice is partly a virtue. He would not understand those elements in the English which balance snobbishness and make it human: the great kindness of the English, their hospitality, their unconscious poetry, their sentimental conservatism, which really admires the gentry. The French Royalist sees that the English like their King. But he does not grasp that while it is base to worship a King, it is almost noble to worship a powerless King. The impotence of the Hanoverian Sovereigns has raised the English loyal subject almost to the chivalry and dignity of a Jacobite. The Frenchman sees that the English servant is respectful: he does not realise that he is also disrespectful; that there is an English legend of the humorous and faithful servant, who is as much a personality as his master; the Caleb Balderstone, the Sam Weller. He sees that the English do admire a nobleman; he does not allow for the fact that they admire a nobleman most when he does not behave like one. They like a noble to be unconscious and amiable: the slave may be humble, but the master must not be proud. The master is Life, as they would like to enjoy it; and among the joys they desire in him there is none which they desire more sincerely than that of generosity, of throwing money about among mankind, or, to use the noble mediæval word, largesse—the joy of largeness. That is why a cabman tells you are no gentleman if you give him his correct fare. Not only his pocket, but his soul is hurt. You have wounded his ideal. You have defaced his vision of the perfect aristocrat. All this is really very subtle and elusive; it is very difficult to separate what is mere slavishness from what is a sort of vicarious nobility in the English love of a lord. And no Frenchman could easily grasp it at all. He would think it was mere slavishness; and if he liked it, he would be a slave. So every Englishman must (at first) feel French candour to be mere brutality. And if he likes it, he is a brute. These national merits must not be understood so easily. It requires long years of plenitude and quiet, the slow growth of great parks, the seasoning of oaken beams, the dark enrichment of red wine in cellars and in inns, all the leisure and the life of England through many centuries, to produce at last the generous and genial fruit of English snobbishness. And it requires battery and barricade, songs in the streets, and ragged men dead for an idea, to produce and justify the terrible flower of French indecency.

When I was in Paris a short time ago, I went with an English friend of mine to an extremely brilliant and rapid succession of French plays, each occupying about twenty minutes. They were all astonishingly effective; but there was one of them which was so effective that my friend and I fought about it outside, and had almost to be separated by the police. It was intended to indicate how men really behaved in a wreck or naval disaster, how they break down, how they scream, how they fight each other without object and in a mere hatred of everything. And then there was added, with all that horrible irony which Voltaire began, a scene in which a great statesman made a speech over their bodies, saying that they were all heroes and had died in a fraternal embrace. My friend and I came out of this theatre, and as he had lived long in Paris, he said, like a Frenchman: "What admirable artistic arrangement! Is it not exquisite?" "No," I replied, assuming as far as possible the traditional attitude of John Bull in the pictures in *Punch*—"No, it is not exquisite. Perhaps it is unmeaning; if it is unmeaning I do not mind. But if it has a meaning I know what the meaning is; it is that under all their pageant of chivalry men are not only beasts, but even hunted beasts. I do not know much of humanity, especially when humanity talks in French. But I know when a thing is meant to uplift the human soul, and when it is meant to depress it. I know that 'Cyrano de Bergerac' (where the actors talked even quicker) was meant to encourage man. And I know that this was meant to discourage him." "These sentimental and moral views of art," began my friend, but I broke into his words as a light broke into my mind. "Let me say to you," I said, "what Jaurès said to Liebknecht at the Socialist Conference: 'You have not died on the barricades'. You are an Englishman, as I am, and you ought to be as amiable as I am. These people have some right to be terrible in art, for they have been terrible in politics. They may endure mock tortures on the stage; they have seen real tortures in the streets. They have been hurt for the idea of Democracy. They have been hurt for the idea of Catholicism. It is not so utterly unnatural to them that they should be hurt for the idea of literature. But, by blazes, it is altogether unnatural to me! And the worst thing of all is that I, who am an Englishman, loving comfort, should find comfort in such things as this. The French do not seek comfort here, but rather unrest. This restless people seeks to keep itself in a perpetual agony of the revolutionary mood. Frenchmen, seeking revolution, may find the humiliation of humanity inspiring. But God forbid that two pleasure-seeking Englishmen should ever find it pleasant!"

THE ZOLA CONTROVERSY

The difference between two great nations can be illustrated by the coincidence that at this moment both France and England are engaged in discussing the memorial of a literary man. France is considering the celebration of the late Zola, England is considering that of the recently deceased Shakspere. There is some national significance, it may be, in the time that has elapsed. Some will find impatience and indelicacy in this early attack on Zola or deification of him; but the nation which has

16

sat still for three hundred years after Shakspere's funeral may be considered, perhaps, to have carried delicacy too far. But much deeper things are involved than the mere matter of time. The point of the contrast is that the French are discussing whether there shall be any monument, while the English are discussing only what the monument shall be. In other words, the French are discussing a living question, while we are discussing a dead one. Or rather, not a dead one, but a settled one, which is quite a different thing.

When a thing of the intellect is settled it is not dead: rather it is immortal. The multiplication table is immortal, and so is the fame of Shakspere. But the fame of Zola is not dead or not immortal; it is at its crisis, it is in the balance; and may be found wanting. The French, therefore, are quite right in considering it a living question. It is still living as a question, because it is not yet solved. But Shakspere is not a living question: he is a living answer.

For my part, therefore, I think the French Zola controversy much more practical and exciting than the English Shakspere one. The admission of Zola to the Pantheon may be regarded as defining Zola's position. But nobody could say that a statue of Shakspere, even fifty feet high, on the top of St. Paul's Cathedral, could define Shakspere's position. It only defines our position towards Shakspere. It is he who is fixed; it is we who are unstable. The nearest approach to an English parallel to the Zola case would be furnished if it were proposed to put some savagely controversial and largely repulsive author among the ashes of the greatest English poets. Suppose, for instance, it were proposed to bury Mr. Rudyard Kipling in Westminster Abbey. I should be against burying him in Westminster Abbey; first, because he is still alive (and here I think even he himself might admit the justice of my protest); and second, because I should like to reserve that rapidly narrowing space for the great permanent examples, not for the interesting foreign interruptions, of English literature. I would not have either Mr. Kipling or Mr. George Moore in Westminster Abbey, though Mr. Kipling has certainly caught even more cleverly than Mr. Moore the lucid and cool cruelty of the French short story. I am very sure that Geoffrey Chaucer and Joseph Addison get on very well together in the Poets' Corner, despite the centuries that sunder them. But I feel that Mr. George Moore would be much happier in Pere-la-Chaise, with a riotous statue by Rodin on the top of him; and Mr. Kipling much happier under some huge Asiatic monument, carved with all the cruelties of the gods.

As to the affair of the English monument to Shakspere, every people has its own mode of commemoration, and I think there is a great deal to be said for ours. There is the French monumental style, which consists in erecting very pompous statues, very well done. There is the German monumental style, which consists in erecting very pompous statues, badly done. And there is the English monumental method, the great English way with statues, which consists in not erecting them at all. A statue may be dignified; but the absence of a statue is always dignified. For my part, I feel there is something national, something wholesomely symbolic, in the fact that there is no statue of Shakspere. There is, of course, one in Leicester Square; but the very place where it stands shows that it was put up by a foreigner for foreigners. There is surely something modest and manly about not attempting to express our greatest poet in the plastic arts in which we do not excel. We honour Shakspere as the Jews honour God—by not daring to make of him a graven image. Our sculpture, our statues, are good enough for bankers and philanthropists, who are our curse: not good enough for him, who is our benediction. Why should we celebrate the very art in which we triumph by the very art in which we fail?

England is most easily understood as the country of amateurs. It is especially the country of amateur soldiers (that is, of Volunteers), of amateur statesmen (that is, of aristocrats), and it is not unreasonable or out of keeping that it should be rather specially the country of a careless and lounging view of literature. Shakspere has no academic monument for the same reason that he had no academic education. He had small Latin and less Greek, and (in the same spirit) he has never been commemorated in Latin epitaphs or Greek marble. If there is nothing clear and fixed about the emblems of his fame, it is because there was nothing clear and fixed about the origins of it. Those great schools and Universities which watch a man in his youth may record him in his death; but Shakspere had no such unifying traditions. We can only say of him what we can say of Dickens. We can only say that he came from nowhere and that he went everywhere. For him a monument in any place is out of place. A cold statue in a certain square is unsuitable to him as it would be unsuitable to Dickens. If we put up a statue of Dickens in Portland Place to-morrow we should feel the stiffness as unnatural. We should fear that the statue might stroll about the street at night.

But in France the question of whether Zola shall go to the Panthéon when he is dead is quite as practicable as the question whether he should go to prison when he was alive. It is the problem of whether the nation shall take one turn of thought or another. In raising a monument to Zola they do not raise merely a trophy, but a finger-post. The question is one which will have to be settled in most European countries; but like all such questions, it has come first to a head in France; because France is the battlefield of Christendom. That question is, of course, roughly this: whether in that ill-defined area of verbal licence on certain dangerous topics it is an extenuation of indelicacy or an aggravation of it that the indelicacy was deliberate and solemn. Is indecency more indecent if it is grave, or more

17

indecent if it is gay? For my part, I belong to an old school in this matter. When a book or a play strikes me as a crime, I am not disarmed by being told that it is a serious crime. If a man has written something vile, I am not comforted by the explanation that he quite meant to do it. I know all the evils of flippancy; I do not like the man who laughs at the sight of virtue. But I prefer him to the man who weeps at the sight of virtue and complains bitterly of there being any such thing. I am not reassured, when ethics are as wild as cannibalism, by the fact that they are also as grave and sincere as suicide. And I think there is an obvious fallacy in the bitter contrasts drawn by some moderns between the aversion to Ibsen's "Ghosts" and the popularity of some such joke as "Dear Old Charlie." Surely there is nothing mysterious or unphilosophic in the popular preference. The joke of "Dear Old Charlie" is passed—because it is a joke. "Ghosts" are exorcised—because they are ghosts.

This is, of course, the whole question of Zola. I am grown up, and I do not worry myself much about Zola's immorality. The thing I cannot stand is his morality. If ever a man on this earth lived to embody the tremendous text, "But if the light in your body be darkness, how great is the darkness," it was certainly he. Great men like Ariosto, Rabelais, and Shakspere fall in foul places, flounder in violent but venial sin, sprawl for pages, exposing their gigantic weakness, are dirty, are indefensible; and then they struggle up again and can still speak with a convincing kindness and an unbroken honour of the best things in the world: Rabelais, of the instruction of ardent and austere youth; Ariosto, of holy chivalry; Shakspere, of the splendid stillness of mercy. But in Zola even the ideals are undesirable; Zola's mercy is colder than justice—nay, Zola's mercy is more bitter in the mouth than injustice. When Zola shows us an ideal training he does not take us, like Rabelais, into the happy fields of humanist learning. He takes us into the schools of inhumanist learning, where there are neither books nor flowers, nor wine nor wisdom, but only deformities in glass bottles, and where the rule is taught from the exceptions. Zola's truth answers the exact description of the skeleton in the cupboard; that is, it is something of which a domestic custom forbids the discovery, but which is quite dead, even when it is discovered. Macaulay said that the Puritans hated bear-baiting, not because it gave pain to the bear, but because it gave pleasure to the spectators. Of such substance also was this Puritan who had lost his God. A Puritan of this type is worse than the Puritan who hates pleasure because there is evil in it. This man actually hates evil because there is pleasure in it. Zola was worse than a pornographer, he was a pessimist. He did worse than encourage sin: he encouraged discouragement. He made lust loathsome because to him lust meant life.

OXFORD FROM WITHOUT

Some time ago I ventured to defend that race of hunted and persecuted outlaws, the Bishops; but until this week I had no idea of how much persecuted they were. For instance, the Bishop of Birmingham made some extremely sensible remarks in the House of Lords, to the effect that Oxford and Cambridge were (as everybody knows they are) far too much merely plutocratic playgrounds. One would have thought that an Anglican Bishop might be allowed to know something about the English University system, and even to have, if anything, some bias in its favour. But (as I pointed out) the rollicking Radicalism of Bishops has to be restrained. The man who writes the notes in the weekly paper called the *Outlook* feels that it is his business to restrain it. The passage has such simple sublimity that I must quote it—

"Dr. Gore talked unworthily of his reputation when he spoke of the older Universities as playgrounds for the rich and idle. In the first place, the rich men there are not idle. Some of the rich men are, and so are some of the poor men. On the whole, the sons of noble and wealthy families keep up the best traditions of academic life."

So far this seems all very nice. It is a part of the universal principle on which Englishmen have acted in recent years. As you will not try to make the best people the most powerful people, persuade yourselves that the most powerful people are the best people. Mad Frenchmen and Irishmen try to realise the ideal. To you belongs the nobler (and much easier) task of idealising the real. First give your Universities entirely into the power of the rich; then let the rich start traditions; and then congratulate yourselves on the fact that the sons of the rich keep up these traditions. All that is quite simple and jolly. But then this critic, who crushes Dr. Gore from the high throne of the *Outlook*, goes on in a way that is really perplexing. "It is distinctly advantageous," he says, "that rich and poor—*i. e.*, young men with a smooth path in life before them, and those who have to hew out a road for themselves—should be brought into association. Each class learns a great deal from the other. On the one side, social conceit and exclusiveness give way to the free spirit of competition amongst all classes; on the other side, angularities and prejudices are rubbed away." Even this I might have swallowed. But the paragraph concludes with this extraordinary sentence: "We get the net result in such careers as those of Lord Milner, Lord Curzon, and Mr. Asquith."

Those three names lay my intellect prostrate. The rest of the argument I understand quite well. The social exclusiveness of aristocrats at Oxford and Cambridge gives way before the free spirit of competition amongst all classes. That is to say, there is at Oxford so hot and keen a struggle, consisting of coal-heavers, London clerks, gypsies, navvies, drapers' assistants, grocers' assistants—

in short, all the classes that make up the bulk of England—there is such a fierce competition at Oxford among all these people that in its presence aristocratic exclusiveness gives way. That is all quite clear. I am not quite sure about the facts, but I quite understand the argument. But then, having been called upon to contemplate this bracing picture of a boisterous turmoil of all the classes of England, I am suddenly asked to accept as example of it, Lord Milner, Lord Curzon, and the present Chancellor of the Exchequer. What part do these gentlemen play in the mental process? Is Lord Curzon one of the rugged and ragged poor men whose angularities have been rubbed away? Or is he one of those whom Oxford immediately deprived of all kind of social exclusiveness? His Oxford reputation does not seem to bear out either account of him. To regard Lord Milner as a typical product of Oxford would surely be unfair. It would be to deprive the educational tradition of Germany of one of its most typical products. English aristocrats have their faults, but they are not at all like Lord Milner. What Mr. Asquith was meant to prove, whether he was a rich man who lost his exclusiveness, or a poor man who lost his angles, I am utterly unable to conceive.

There is, however, one mild but very evident truth that might perhaps be mentioned. And it is this: that none of those three excellent persons is, or ever has been, a poor man in the sense that that word is understood by the overwhelming majority of the English nation. There are no poor men at Oxford in the sense that the majority of men in the street are poor. The very fact that the writer in the *Outlook* can talk about such people as poor shows that he does not understand what the modern problem is. His kind of poor man rather reminds me of the Earl in the ballad by that great English satirist, Sir W.S. Gilbert, whose angles (very acute angles) had, I fear, never been rubbed down by an old English University. The reader will remember that when the Periwinkle-girl was adored by two Dukes, the poet added—
"A third adorer had the girl,
A man of lowly station;
A miserable grovelling Earl
Besought her approbation."
Perhaps, indeed, some allusion to our University system, and to the universal clash in it of all the classes of the community, may be found in the verse a little farther on, which says—
"He'd had, it happily befell,
A decent education;
His views would have befitted well
A far superior station."
Possibly there was as simple a chasm between Lord Curzon and Lord Milner. But I am afraid that the chasm will become almost imperceptible, a microscopic crack, if we compare it with the chasm that separates either or both of them from the people of this country.

Of course the truth is exactly as the Bishop of Birmingham put it. I am sure that he did not put it in any unkindly or contemptuous spirit towards those old English seats of learning, which whether they are or are not seats of learning, are, at any rate, old and English, and those are two very good things to be. The Old English University is a playground for the governing class. That does not prove that it is a bad thing; it might prove that it was a very good thing. Certainly if there is a governing class, let there be a playground for the governing class. I would much rather be ruled by men who know how to play than by men who do not know how to play. Granted that we are to be governed by a rich section of the community, it is certainly very important that that section should be kept tolerably genial and jolly. If the sensitive man on the *Outlook* does not like the phrase, "Playground of the rich," I can suggest a phrase that describes such a place as Oxford perhaps with more precision. It is a place for humanising those who might otherwise be tyrants, or even experts.

To pretend that the aristocrat meets all classes at Oxford is too ludicrous to be worth discussion. But it may be true that he meets more different kinds of men than he would meet under a strictly aristocratic *regime* of private tutors and small schools. It all comes back to the fact that the English, if they were resolved to have an aristocracy, were at least resolved to have a good-natured aristocracy. And it is due to them to say that almost alone among the peoples of the world, they have succeeded in getting one. One could almost tolerate the thing, if it were not for the praise of it. One might endure Oxford, but not the *Outlook*.

When the poor man at Oxford loses his angles (which means, I suppose, his independence), he may perhaps, even if his poverty is of that highly relative type possible at Oxford, gain a certain amount of worldly advantage from the surrender of those angles. I must confess, however, that I can imagine nothing nastier than to lose one's angles. It seems to me that a desire to retain some angles about one's person is a desire common to all those human beings who do not set their ultimate hopes upon looking like Humpty-Dumpty. Our angles are simply our shapes. I cannot imagine any phrase more full of the subtle and exquisite vileness which is poisoning and weakening our country than such a phrase as this, about the desirability of rubbing down the angularities of poor men. Reduced to permanent and practical human speech, it means nothing whatever except the corrupting of that first human sense of justice which is the critic of all human institutions.

19

It is not in any such spirit of facile and reckless reassurance that we should approach the really difficult problem of the delicate virtues and the deep dangers of our two historic seats of learning. A good son does not easily admit that his sick mother is dying; but neither does a good son cheerily assert that she is "all right." There are many good arguments for leaving the two historic Universities exactly as they are. There are many good arguments for smashing them or altering them entirely. But in either case the plain truth told by the Bishop of Birmingham remains. If these Universities were destroyed, they would not be destroyed as Universities. If they are preserved, they will not be preserved as Universities. They will be preserved strictly and literally as playgrounds; places valued for their hours of leisure more than for their hours of work. I do not say that this is unreasonable; as a matter of private temperament I find it attractive. It is not only possible to say a great deal in praise of play; it is really possible to say the highest things in praise of it. It might reasonably be maintained that the true object of all human life is play. Earth is a task garden; heaven is a playground. To be at last in such secure innocence that one can juggle with the universe and the stars, to be so good that one can treat everything as a joke—that may be, perhaps, the real end and final holiday of human souls. When we are really holy we may regard the Universe as a lark; so perhaps it is not essentially wrong to regard the University as a lark. But the plain and present fact is that our upper classes do regard the University as a lark, and do not regard it as a University. It also happens very often that through some oversight they neglect to provide themselves with that extreme degree of holiness which I have postulated as a necessary preliminary to such indulgence in the higher frivolity.

Humanity, always dreaming of a happy race, free, fantastic, and at ease, has sometimes pictured them in some mystical island, sometimes in some celestial city, sometimes as fairies, gods, or citizens of Atlantis. But one method in which it has often indulged is to picture them as aristocrats, as a special human class that could actually be seen hunting in the woods or driving about the streets. And this never was (as some silly Germans say) a worship of pride and scorn; mankind never really admired pride; mankind never had any thing but a scorn for scorn. It was a worship of the spectacle of happiness; especially of the spectacle of youth. This is what the old Universities in their noblest aspect really are; and this is why there is always something to be said for keeping them as they are. Aristocracy is not a tyranny; it is not even merely a spell. It is a vision. It is a deliberate indulgence in a certain picture of pleasure painted for the purpose; every Duchess is (in an innocent sense) painted, like Gainsborough's "Duchess of Devonshire." She is only beautiful because, at the back of all, the English people wanted her to be beautiful. In the same way, the lads at Oxford and Cambridge are only larking because England, in the depths of its solemn soul, really wishes them to lark. All this is very human and pardonable, and would be even harmless if there were no such things in the world as danger and honour and intellectual responsibility. But if aristocracy is a vision, it is perhaps the most unpractical of all visions. It is not a working way of doing things to put all your happiest people on a lighted platform and stare only at them. It is not a working way of managing education to be entirely content with the mere fact that you have (to a degree unexampled in the world) given the luckiest boys the jolliest time. It would be easy enough, like the writer in the *Outlook*, to enjoy the pleasures and deny the perils. Oh what a happy place England would be to live in if only one did not love it!

WOMAN

A correspondent has written me an able and interesting letter in the matter of some allusions of mine to the subject of communal kitchens. He defends communal kitchens very lucidly from the standpoint of the calculating collectivist; but, like many of his school, he cannot apparently grasp that there is another test of the whole matter, with which such calculation has nothing at all to do. He knows it would be cheaper if a number of us ate at the same time, so as to use the same table. So it would. It would also be cheaper if a number of us slept at different times, so as to use the same pair of trousers. But the question is not how cheap are we buying a thing, but what are we buying? It is cheap to own a slave. And it is cheaper still to be a slave.

My correspondent also says that the habit of dining out in restaurants, etc., is growing. So, I believe, is the habit of committing suicide. I do not desire to connect the two facts together. It seems fairly clear that a man could not dine at a restaurant because he had just committed suicide; and it would be extreme, perhaps, to suggest that he commits suicide because he has just dined at a restaurant. But the two cases, when put side by side, are enough to indicate the falsity and poltroonery of this eternal modern argument from what is in fashion. The question for brave men is not whether a certain thing is increasing; the question is whether we are increasing it. I dine very often in restaurants because the nature of my trade makes it convenient: but if I thought that by dining in restaurants I was working for the creation of communal meals, I would never enter a restaurant again; I would carry bread and cheese in my pocket or eat chocolate out of automatic machines. For the personal element in some things is sacred. I heard Mr. Will Crooks put it perfectly the other day: "The most sacred thing is to be able to shut your own door."

My correspondent says, "Would not our women be spared the drudgery of cooking and all its attendant worries, leaving them free for higher culture?" The first thing that occurs to me to say about this is very simple, and is, I imagine, a part of all our experience. If my correspondent can find any way of preventing women from worrying, he will indeed be a remarkable man. I think the matter is a much deeper one. First of all, my correspondent overlooks a distinction which is elementary in our human nature. Theoretically, I suppose, every one would like to be freed from worries. But nobody in the world would always like to be freed from worrying occupations. I should very much like (as far as my feelings at the moment go) to be free from the consuming nuisance of writing this article. But it does not follow that I should like to be free from the consuming nuisance of being a journalist. Because we are worried about a thing, it does not follow that we are not interested in it. The truth is the other way. If we are not interested, why on earth should we be worried? Women are worried about housekeeping, but those that are most interested are the most worried. Women are still more worried about their husbands and their children. And I suppose if we strangled the children and poleaxed the husbands it would leave women free for higher culture. That is, it would leave them free to begin to worry about that. For women would worry about higher culture as much as they worry about everything else.

I believe this way of talking about women and their higher culture is almost entirely a growth of the classes which (unlike the journalistic class to which I belong) have always a reasonable amount of money. One odd thing I specially notice. Those who write like this seem entirely to forget the existence of the working and wage-earning classes. They say eternally, like my correspondent, that the ordinary woman is always a drudge. And what, in the name of the Nine Gods, is the ordinary man? These people seem to think that the ordinary man is a Cabinet Minister. They are always talking about man going forth to wield power, to carve his own way, to stamp his individuality on the world, to command and to be obeyed. This may be true of a certain class. Dukes, perhaps, are not drudges; but, then, neither are Duchesses. The Ladies and Gentlemen of the Smart Set are quite free for the higher culture, which consists chiefly of motoring and Bridge. But the ordinary man who typifies and constitutes the millions that make up our civilisation is no more free for the higher culture than his wife is.

Indeed, he is not so free. Of the two sexes the woman is in the more powerful position. For the average woman is at the head of something with which she can do as she likes; the average man has to obey orders and do nothing else. He has to put one dull brick on another dull brick, and do nothing else; he has to add one dull figure to another dull figure, and do nothing else. The woman's world is a small one, perhaps, but she can alter it. The woman can tell the tradesman with whom she deals some realistic things about himself. The clerk who does this to the manager generally gets the sack, or shall we say (to avoid the vulgarism), finds himself free for higher culture. Above all, as I said in my previous article, the woman does work which is in some small degree creative and individual. She can put the flowers or the furniture in fancy arrangements of her own. I fear the bricklayer cannot put the bricks in fancy arrangements of his own, without disaster to himself and others. If the woman is only putting a patch into a carpet, she can choose the thing with regard to colour. I fear it would not do for the office boy dispatching a parcel to choose his stamps with a view to colour; to prefer the tender mauve of the sixpenny to the crude scarlet of the penny stamp. A woman cooking may not always cook artistically; still she can cook artistically. She can introduce a personal and imperceptible alteration into the composition of a soup. The clerk is not encouraged to introduce a personal and imperceptible alteration into the figures in a ledger.

The trouble is that the real question I raised is not discussed. It is argued as a problem in pennies, not as a problem in people. It is not the proposals of these reformers that I feel to be false so much as their temper and their arguments. I am not nearly so certain that communal kitchens are wrong as I am that the defenders of communal kitchens are wrong. Of course, for one thing, there is a vast difference between the communal kitchens of which I spoke and the communal meal (*monstrum horrendum, informe*) which the darker and wilder mind of my correspondent diabolically calls up. But in both the trouble is that their defenders will not defend them humanly as human institutions. They will not interest themselves in the staring psychological fact that there are some things that a man or a woman, as the case may be, wishes to do for himself or herself. He or she must do it inventively, creatively, artistically, individually—in a word, badly. Choosing your wife (say) is one of these things. Is choosing your husband's dinner one of these things? That is the whole question: it is never asked.

And then the higher culture. I know that culture. I would not set any man free for it if I could help it. The effect of it on the rich men who are free for it is so horrible that it is worse than any of the other amusements of the millionaire—worse than gambling, worse even than philanthropy. It means thinking the smallest poet in Belgium greater than the greatest poet of England. It means losing every democratic sympathy. It means being unable to talk to a navvy about sport, or about beer, or about the Bible, or about the Derby, or about patriotism, or about anything whatever that he, the navvy, wants to talk about. It means taking literature seriously, a very amateurish thing to do. It means pardoning indecency only when it is gloomy indecency. Its disciples will call a spade a spade; but only when it is a grave-digger's spade. The higher culture is sad, cheap, impudent, unkind, without

21

honesty and without ease. In short, it is "high." That abominable word (also applied to game) admirably describes it.

No; if you were setting women free for something else, I might be more melted. If you can assure me, privately and gravely, that you are setting women free to dance on the mountains like mænads, or to worship some monstrous goddess, I will make a note of your request. If you are quite sure that the ladies in Brixton, the moment they give up cooking, will beat great gongs and blow horns to Mumbo-Jumbo, then I will agree that the occupation is at least human and is more or less entertaining. Women have been set free to be Bacchantes; they have been set free to be Virgin Martyrs; they have been set free to be Witches. Do not ask them now to sink so low as the higher culture.

I have my own little notions of the possible emancipation of women; but I suppose I should not be taken very seriously if I propounded them. I should favour anything that would increase the present enormous authority of women and their creative action in their own homes. The average woman, as I have said, is a despot; the average man is a serf. I am for any scheme that any one can suggest that will make the average woman more of a despot. So far from wishing her to get her cooked meals from outside, I should like her to cook more wildly and at her own will than she does. So far from getting always the same meals from the same place, let her invent, if she likes, a new dish every day of her life. Let woman be more of a maker, not less. We are right to talk about "Woman;" only blackguards talk about women. Yet all men talk about men, and that is the whole difference. Men represent the deliberative and democratic element in life. Woman represents the despotic.

THE MODERN MARTYR

The incident of the Suffragettes who chained themselves with iron chains to the railings of Downing Street is a good ironical allegory of most modern martyrdom. It generally consists of a man chaining himself up and then complaining that he is not free. Some say that such larks retard the cause of female suffrage, others say that such larks alone can advance it; as a matter of fact, I do not believe that they have the smallest effect one way or the other.

The modern notion of impressing the public by a mere demonstration of unpopularity, by being thrown out of meetings or thrown into jail is largely a mistake. It rests on a fallacy touching the true popular value of martyrdom. People look at human history and see that it has often happened that persecutions have not only advertised but even advanced a persecuted creed, and given to its validity the public and dreadful witness of dying men. The paradox was pictorially expressed in Christian art, in which saints were shown brandishing as weapons the very tools that had slain them. And because his martyrdom is thus a power to the martyr, modern people think that any one who makes himself slightly uncomfortable in public will immediately be uproariously popular. This element of inadequate martyrdom is not true only of the Suffragettes; it is true of many movements I respect and some that I agree with. It was true, for instance, of the Passive Resisters, who had pieces of their furniture sold up. The assumption is that if you show your ordinary sincerity (or even your political ambition) by being a nuisance to yourself as well as to other people, you will have the strength of the great saints who passed through the fire. Any one who can be hustled in a hall for five minutes, or put in a cell for five days, has achieved what was meant by martyrdom, and has a halo in the Christian art of the future. Miss Pankhurst will be represented holding a policeman in each hand—the instruments of her martyrdom. The Passive Resister will be shown symbolically carrying the teapot that was torn from him by tyrannical auctioneers.

But there is a fallacy in this analogy of martyrdom. The truth is that the special impressiveness which does come from being persecuted only happens in the case of extreme persecution. For the fact that the modern enthusiast will undergo some inconvenience for the creed he holds only proves that he does hold it, which no one ever doubted. No one doubts that the Nonconformist minister cares more for Nonconformity than he does for his teapot. No one doubts that Miss Pankhurst wants a vote more than she wants a quiet afternoon and an armchair. All our ordinary intellectual opinions are worth a bit of a row: I remember during the Boer War fighting an Imperialist clerk outside the Queen's Hall, and giving and receiving a bloody nose; but I did not think it one of the incidents that produce the psychological effect of the Roman amphitheatre or the stake at Smithfield. For in that impression there is something more than the mere fact that a man is sincere enough to give his time or his comfort. Pagans were not impressed by the torture of Christians merely because it showed that they honestly held their opinion; they knew that millions of people honestly held all sorts of opinions. The point of such extreme martyrdom is much more subtle. It is that it gives an appearance of a man having something quite specially strong to back him up, of his drawing upon some power. And this can only be proved when all his physical contentment is destroyed; when all the current of his bodily being is reversed and turned to pain. If a man is seen to be roaring with laughter all the time that he is skinned alive, it would not be unreasonable to deduce that somewhere in the recesses of his mind he had thought of a rather good joke. Similarly, if men smiled and sang (as they did) while they were being boiled or torn in pieces, the spectators felt the presence of something more than mere mental honesty: they felt the presence of some new and unintelligible kind of pleasure, which, presumably, came from somewhere. It might be a strength of madness, or a lying spirit from Hell; but it was something quite positive and extraordinary; as positive as brandy and as extraordinary as conjuring. The Pagan said to himself: "If Christianity makes a man happy while his legs are being eaten by a lion, might it not make me happy while my legs are still attached to me and walking down the street?" The Secularists laboriously explain that martyrdoms do not prove a faith to be true, as if anybody was ever such a fool as to suppose that they did. What they did prove, or, rather, strongly suggest, was that something had entered human psychology which was stronger than strong pain. If a young girl, scourged and bleeding to death, saw nothing but a crown descending on her from God, the first mental step was not that her philosophy was correct, but that she was certainly feeding on something. But this particular point of psychology does not arise at all in the modern cases of mere public discomfort or inconvenience. The causes of Miss Pankhurst's cheerfulness require no mystical explanations. If she were being burned alive as a witch, if she then looked up in unmixed rapture and saw a ballot-box descending out of heaven, then I should say that the incident, though not conclusive, was frightfully impressive. It would not prove logically that she ought to have the vote, or that anybody ought to have the vote. But it would prove this: that there was, for some reason, a sacramental reality in the vote, that the soul could take the vote and feed on it; that it was in itself a positive and overpowering pleasure, capable of being pitted against positive and overpowering pain.

I should advise modern agitators, therefore, to give up this particular method: the method of making very big efforts to get a very small punishment. It does not really go down at all; the punishment is too small, and the efforts are too obvious. It has not any of the effectiveness of the old savage martyrdom, because it does not leave the victim absolutely alone with his cause, so that his cause alone can support him. At the same time it has about it that element of the pantomimic and the absurd, which was the cruellest part of the slaying and the mocking of the real prophets. St. Peter was crucified upside down as a huge inhuman joke; but his human seriousness survived the inhuman joke, because, in whatever posture, he had died for his faith. The modern martyr of the Pankhurst type courts the absurdity without making the suffering strong enough to eclipse the absurdity. She is like a St. Peter who should deliberately stand on his head for ten seconds and then expect to be canonised for it.

Or, again, the matter might be put in this way. Modern martyrdoms fail even as demonstrations, because they do not prove even that the martyrs are completely serious. I think, as a fact, that the modern martyrs generally are serious, perhaps a trifle too serious. But their martyrdom does not prove it; and the public does not always believe it. Undoubtedly, as a fact, Dr. Clifford is quite honourably indignant with what he considers to be clericalism, but he does not prove it by having his teapot sold; for a man might easily have his teapot sold as an actress has her diamonds stolen—as a personal advertisement. As a matter of fact, Miss Pankhurst is quite in earnest about votes for women. But she does not prove it by being chucked out of meetings. A person might be chucked out of meetings just as young men are chucked out of music-halls—for fun. But no man has himself eaten by a lion as a personal advertisement. No woman is broiled on a gridiron for fun. That is where the testimony of St. Perpetua and St. Faith comes in. Doubtless it is no fault of these enthusiasts that they are not subjected to the old and searching penalties; very likely they would pass through them as triumphantly as St. Agatha. I am simply advising them upon a point of policy, things being as they are. And I say that the average man is not impressed with their sacrifices simply because they are not and cannot be more decisive than the sacrifices which the average man himself would make for mere fun if he were drunk. Drunkards would interrupt meetings and take the consequences. And as for selling a teapot, it is an act, I imagine, in which any properly constituted drunkard would take a positive pleasure. The advertisement is not good enough; it does not tell. If I were really martyred for an opinion (which is more improbable than words can say), it would certainly only be for one or two of my most central and sacred opinions. I might, perhaps, be shot for England, but certainly not for the British Empire. I might conceivably die for political freedom, but I certainly wouldn't die for Free Trade. But as for kicking up the particular kind of shindy that the Suffragettes are kicking up, I would as soon do it for my shallowest opinion as for my deepest one. It never could be anything worse than an inconvenience; it never could be anything better than a spree. Hence the British public, and especially the working classes, regard the whole demonstration with fundamental indifference; for, while it is a demonstration that probably is adopted from the most fanatical motives, it is a demonstration which might be adopted from the most frivolous.

ON POLITICAL SECRECY

Generally, instinctively, in the absence of any special reason, humanity hates the idea of anything being hidden—that is, it hates the idea of anything being successfully hidden. Hide-and-seek is a popular pastime; but it assumes the truth of the text, "Seek and ye shall find." Ordinary mankind (gigantic and unconquerable in its power of joy) can get a great deal of pleasure out of a game called "hide the thimble," but that is only because it is really a game of "see the thimble." Suppose that at the end of such a game the thimble had not been found at all; suppose its place was unknown for ever: the result on the players would not be playful, it would be tragic. That thimble would hag-ride all their dreams. They would all die in asylums. The pleasure is all in the poignant moment of passing from not knowing to knowing. Mystery stories are very popular, especially when sold at sixpence; but that is because the author of a mystery story reveals. He is enjoyed not because he creates mystery, but because he destroys mystery. Nobody would have the courage to publish a detective-story which left the problem exactly where it found it. That would rouse even the London public to revolution. No one dare publish a detective-story that did not detect.

There are three broad classes of the special things in which human wisdom does permit privacy. The first is the case I have mentioned—that of hide-and-seek, or the police novel, in which it permits privacy only in order to explode and smash privacy. The author makes first a fastidious secret of how the Bishop was murdered, only in order that he may at last declare, as from a high tower, to the whole democracy the great glad news that he was murdered by the governess. In that case, ignorance is only valued because being ignorant is the best and purest preparation for receiving the horrible revelations of high life. Somewhat in the same way being an agnostic is the best and purest preparation for receiving the happy revelations of St. John.

This first sort of secrecy we may dismiss, for its whole ultimate object is not to keep the secret, but to tell it. Then there is a second and far more important class of things which humanity does agree to hide. They are so important that they cannot possibly be discussed here. But every one will know the kind of things I mean. In connection with these, I wish to remark that though they are, in one sense, a secret, they are also always a "sécret de Polichinelle." Upon sex and such matters we are in a human freemasonry; the freemasonry is disciplined, but the freemasonry is free. We are asked to be silent about these things, but we are not asked to be ignorant about them. On the contrary, the fundamental human argument is entirely the other way. It is the thing most common to humanity that is most veiled by humanity. It is exactly because we all know that it is there that we need not say that it is there.

Then there is a third class of things on which the best civilisation does permit privacy, does resent all inquiry or explanation. This is in the case of things which need not be explained, because they cannot be explained, things too airy, instinctive, or intangible—caprices, sudden impulses, and the more innocent kind of prejudice. A man must not be asked why he is talkative or silent, for the simple reason that he does not know. A man is not asked (even in Germany) why he walks slow or quick, simply because he could not answer. A man must take his own road through a wood, and make his own use of a holiday. And the reason is this: not because he has a strong reason, but actually because he has a weak reason; because he has a slight and fleeting feeling about the matter which he could not explain to a policeman, which perhaps the very appearance of a policeman out of the bushes might destroy. He must act on the impulse, because the impulse is unimportant, and he may never have the same impulse again. If you like to put it so he must act on the impulse because the impulse is not worth a moment's thought. All these fancies men feel should be private; and even Fabians have never proposed to interfere with them.

Now, for the last fortnight the newspapers have been full of very varied comments upon the problem of the secrecy of certain parts of our political finance, and especially of the problem of the party funds. Some papers have failed entirely to understand what the quarrel is about. They have urged that Irish members and Labour members are also under the shadow, or, as some have said, even more under it. The ground of this frantic statement seems, when patiently considered, to be simply this: that Irish and Labour members receive money for what they do. All persons, as far as I know, on this earth receive money for what they do; the only difference is that some people, like the Irish members, do it.

I cannot imagine that any human being could think any other human being capable of maintaining the proposition that men ought not to receive money. The simple point is that, as we know that some money is given rightly and some wrongly, an elementary common-sense leads us to look with indifference at the money that is given in the middle of Ludgate Circus, and to look with particular suspicion at the money which a man will not give unless he is shut up in a box or a bathing-machine. In short, it is too silly to suppose that anybody could ever have discussed the desirability of funds. The only thing that even idiots could ever have discussed is the concealment of funds. Therefore, the whole question that we have to consider is whether the concealment of political money-transactions, the purchase of peerages, the payment of election expenses, is a kind of concealment that falls under any of the three classes I have mentioned as those in which human custom and instinct does permit us to conceal. I have suggested three kinds of secrecy which are human and defensible. Can this institution be defended by means of any of them?

Now the question is whether this political secrecy is of any of the kinds that can be called legitimate. We have roughly divided legitimate secrets into three classes. First comes the secret that is only kept in order to be revealed, as in the detective stories; secondly, the secret which is kept

24

because everybody knows it, as in sex; and third, the secret which is kept because it is too delicate and vague to be explained at all, as in the choice of a country walk. Do any of these broad human divisions cover such a case as that of secrecy of the political and party finances? It would be absurd, and even delightfully absurd, to pretend that any of them did. It would be a wild and charming fancy to suggest that our politicians keep political secrets only that they may make political revelations. A modern peer only pretends that he has earned his peerage in order that he may more dramatically declare, with a scream of scorn and joy, that he really bought it. The Baronet pretends that he deserved his title only in order to make more exquisite and startling the grand historical fact that he did not deserve it. Surely this sounds improbable. Surely all our statesmen cannot be saving themselves up for the excitement of a death-bed repentance. The writer of detective tales makes a man a duke solely in order to blast him with a charge of burglary. But surely the Prime Minister does not make a man a duke solely in order to blast him with a charge of bribery. No; the detective-tale theory of the secrecy of political funds must (with a sigh) be given up.

Neither can we say that the thing is explained by that second case of human secrecy which is so secret that it is hard to discuss it in public. A decency is preserved about certain primary human matters precisely because every one knows all about them. But the decency touching contributions, purchases, and peerages is not kept up because most ordinary men know what is happening; it is kept up precisely because most ordinary men do not know what is happening. The ordinary curtain of decorum covers normal proceedings. But no one will say that being bribed is a normal proceeding.

And if we apply the third test to this problem of political secrecy, the case is even clearer and even more funny. Surely no one will say that the purchase of peerages and such things are kept secret because they are so light and impulsive and unimportant that they must be matters of individual fancy. A child sees a flower and for the first time feels inclined to pick it. But surely no one will say that a brewer sees a coronet and for the first time suddenly thinks that he would like to be a peer. The child's impulse need not be explained to the police, for the simple reason that it could not be explained to anybody. But does any one believe that the laborious political ambitions of modern commercial men ever have this airy and incommunicable character? A man lying on the beach may throw stones into the sea without any particular reason. But does any one believe that the brewer throws bags of gold into the party funds without any particular reason? This theory of the secrecy of political money must also be regretfully abandoned; and with it the two other possible excuses as well. This secrecy is one which cannot be justified as a sensational joke nor as a common human freemasonry, nor as an indescribable personal whim. Strangely enough, indeed, it violates all three conditions and classes at once. It is not hidden in order to be revealed: it is hidden in order to be hidden. It is not kept secret because it is a common secret of mankind, but because mankind must not get hold of it. And it is not kept secret because it is too unimportant to be told, but because it is much too important to bear telling. In short, the thing we have is the real and perhaps rare political phenomenon of an occult government. We have an exoteric and an esoteric doctrine. England is really ruled by priestcraft, but not by priests. We have in this country all that has ever been alleged against the evil side of religion; the peculiar class with privileges, the sacred words that are unpronounceable; the important things known only to the few. In fact we lack nothing except the religion.

EDWARD VII. AND SCOTLAND

I have received a serious, and to me, at any rate, an impressive remonstrance from the Scottish Patriotic Association. It appears that I recently referred to Edward VII. of Great Britain and Ireland, King, Defender of the Faith, under the horrible description of the King of England. The Scottish Patriotic Association draws my attention to the fact that by the provisions of the Act of Union, and the tradition of nationality, the monarch should be referred to as the King of Britain. The blow thus struck at me is particularly wounding because it is particularly unjust. I believe in the reality of the independent nationalities under the British Crown much more passionately and positively than any other educated Englishman of my acquaintance believes in it. I am quite certain that Scotland is a nation; I am quite certain that nationality is the key of Scotland; I am quite certain that all our success with Scotland has been due to the fact that we have in spirit treated it as a nation. I am quite certain that Ireland is a nation; I am quite certain that nationality is the key to Ireland; I am quite certain that all our failure in Ireland arose from the fact that we would not in spirit treat it as a nation. It would be difficult to find, even among the innumerable examples that exist, a stronger example of the immensely superior importance of sentiment to what is called practicality than this case of the two sister nations. It is not that we have encouraged a Scotchman to be rich; it is not that we have encouraged a Scotchman to be active; it is not that we have encouraged a Scotchman to be free. It is that we have quite definitely encouraged a Scotchman to be Scotch.

A vague, but vivid impression was received from all our writers of history, philosophy, and rhetoric that the Scottish element was something really valuable in itself, was something which even Englishmen were forced to recognise and respect. If we ever admitted the beauty of Ireland, it was as something which might be loved by an Englishman but which could hardly be respected even by an Irishman. A Scotchman might be proud of Scotland; it was enough for an Irishman that he could be fond of Ireland. Our success with the two nations has been exactly proportioned to our encouragement of their independent national emotion; the one that we would not treat nationally has alone produced Nationalists. The one nation that we would not recognise as a nation in theory is the one that we have been forced to recognise as a nation in arms. The Scottish Patriotic Association has no need to draw my attention to the importance of the separate national sentiment or the need of keeping the Border as a sacred line. The case is quite sufficiently proved by the positive history of Scotland. The place of Scottish loyalty to England has been taken by English admiration of Scotland. They do not need to envy us our titular leadership, when we seem to envy them their separation.

I wish to make very clear my entire sympathy with the national sentiment of the Scottish Patriotic Association. But I wish also to make clear this very enlightening comparison between the fate of Scotch and of Irish patriotism. In life it is always the little facts that express the large emotions, and if the English once respected Ireland as they respect Scotland, it would come out in a hundred small ways. For instance, there are crack regiments in the British Army which wear the kilt—the kilt which, as Macaulay says with perfect truth, was regarded by nine Scotchmen out of ten as the dress of a thief. The Highland officers carry a silver-hilted version of the old barbarous Gaelic broadsword with a basket-hilt, which split the skulls of so many English soldiers at Killiecrankie and Prestonpans. When you have a regiment of men in the British Army carrying ornamental silver shillelaghs you will have done the same thing for Ireland, and not before—or when you mention Brian Boru with the same intonation as Bruce.

Let me be considered therefore to have made quite clear that I believe with a quite special intensity in the independent consideration of Scotland and Ireland as apart from England. I believe that, in the proper sense of the words, Scotland is an independent nation, even if Edward VII. is the King of Scotland. I believe that, in the proper sense of words, Ireland is an independent nation, even if Edward VII. is King of Ireland. But the fact is that I have an even bolder and wilder belief than either of these. I believe that England is an independent nation. I believe that England also has its independent colour and history, and meaning. I believe that England could produce costumes quite as queer as the kilt; I believe that England has heroes fully as untranslateable as Brian Boru, and consequently I believe that Edward VII. is, among his innumerable other functions, really King of England. If my Scotch friends insist, let us call it one of his quite obscure, unpopular, and minor titles; one of his relaxations. A little while ago he was Duke of Cornwall; but for a family accident he might still have been King of Hanover. Nor do I think that we should blame the simple Cornishmen if they spoke of him in a rhetorical moment by his Cornish title, nor the well-meaning Hanoverians if they classed him with Hanoverian Princes.

Now it so happens that in the passage complained of I said the King of England merely because I meant the King of England. I was speaking strictly and especially of English Kings, of Kings in the tradition of the old Kings of England. I wrote as an English nationalist keenly conscious of the sacred boundary of the Tweed that keeps (or used to keep) our ancient enemies at bay. I wrote as an English nationalist resolved for one wild moment to throw off the tyranny of the Scotch and Irish who govern and oppress my country. I felt that England was at least spiritually guarded against these surrounding nationalities. I dreamed that the Tweed was guarded by the ghosts of Scropes and Percys; I dreamed that St. George's Channel was guarded by St. George. And in this insular security I spoke deliberately and specifically of the King of England, of the representative of the Tudors and Plantagenets. It is true that the two Kings of England, of whom I especially spoke, Charles II. and George III., had both an alien origin, not very recent and not very remote. Charles II. came of a family originally Scotch. George III. came of a family originally German. But the same, so far as that goes, could be said of the English royal houses when England stood quite alone. The Plantagenets were originally a French family. The Tudors were originally a Welsh family. But I was not talking of the amount of English sentiment in the English Kings. I was talking of the amount of English sentiment in the English treatment and popularity of the English Kings. With that Ireland and Scotland have nothing whatever to do.

Charles II. may, for all I know, have not only been King of Scotland; he may, by virtue of his temper and ancestry, have been a Scotch King of Scotland. There was something Scotch about his combination of clear-headedness with sensuality. There was something Scotch about his combination of doing what he liked with knowing what he was doing. But I was not talking of the personality of Charles, which may have been Scotch. I was talking of the popularity of Charles, which was certainly English. One thing is quite certain: whether or no he ever ceased to be a Scotch man, he ceased as soon as he conveniently could to be a Scotch King. He had actually tried the experiment of being a national ruler north of the Tweed, and his people liked him as little as he liked them. Of Presbyterianism, of the Scottish religion, he left on record the exquisitely English judgment that it was "no religion for a gentleman." His popularity then was purely English; his royalty was purely English; and I was using the words with the utmost narrowness and deliberation when I spoke of this particular popularity and royalty as the popularity and royalty of a King of England. I said of the English people specially that they like to pick up the King's crown when he has dropped it. I do not feel at all sure that this does apply to the Scotch or the Irish. I think that the Irish would knock his crown off for him. I think that the Scotch would keep it for him after they had picked it up.

For my part, I should be inclined to adopt quite the opposite method of asserting nationality. Why should good Scotch nationalists call Edward VII. the King of Britain? They ought to call him King Edward I. of Scotland. What is Britain? Where is Britain? There is no such place. There never was a nation of Britain; there never was a King of Britain; unless perhaps Vortigern or Uther Pendragon had a taste for the title. If we are to develop our Monarchy, I should be altogether in favour of developing it along the line of local patriotism and of local proprietorship in the King. I think that the Londoners ought to call him the King of London, and the Liverpudlians ought to call him the King of Liverpool. I do not go so far as to say that the people of Birmingham ought to call Edward VII. the King of Birmingham; for that would be high treason to a holier and more established power. But I think we might read in the papers: "The King of Brighton left Brighton at half-past two this afternoon," and then immediately afterwards, "The King of Worthing entered Worthing at ten minutes past three." Or, "The people of Margate bade a reluctant farewell to the popular King of Margate this morning," and then, "His Majesty the King of Ramsgate returned to his country and capital this afternoon after his long sojourn in strange lands." It might be pointed out that by a curious coincidence the departure of the King of Oxford occurred a very short time before the triumphal arrival of the King of Reading. I cannot imagine any method which would more increase the kindly and normal relations between the Sovereign and his people. Nor do I think that such a method would be in any sense a depreciation of the royal dignity; for, as a matter of fact, it would put the King upon the same platform with the gods. The saints, the most exalted of human figures, were also the most local. It was exactly the men whom we most easily connected with heaven whom we also most easily connected with earth.

THOUGHTS AROUND KOEPENICK

A famous and epigrammatic author said that life copied literature; it seems clear that life really caricatures it. I suggested recently that the Germans submitted to, and even admired, a solemn and theatrical assertion of authority. A few hours after I had sent up my "copy," I saw the first announcement of the affair of the comic Captain at Koepenick. The most absurd part of this absurd fraud (at least, to English eyes) is one which, oddly enough, has received comparatively little comment. I mean the point at which the Mayor asked for a warrant, and the Captain pointed to the bayonets of his soldiery and said. "These are my authority." One would have thought any one would have known that no soldier would talk like that. The dupes were blamed for not knowing that the man wore the wrong cap or the wrong sash, or had his sword buckled on the wrong way; but these are technicalities which they might surely be excused for not knowing. I certainly should not know if a soldier's sash were on inside out or his cap on behind before. But I should know uncommonly well that genuine professional soldiers do not talk like Adelphi villains and utter theatrical epigrams in praise of abstract violence.

We can see this more clearly, perhaps, if we suppose it to be the case of any other dignified and clearly distinguishable profession. Suppose a Bishop called upon me. My great modesty and my rather distant reverence for the higher clergy might lead me certainly to a strong suspicion that any Bishop who called on me was a bogus Bishop. But if I wished to test his genuineness I should not dream of attempting to do so by examining the shape of his apron or the way his gaiters were done up. I have not the remotest idea of the way his gaiters ought to be done up. A very vague approximation to an apron would probably take me in; and if he behaved like an approximately Christian gentleman he would be safe enough from my detection. But suppose the Bishop, the moment he entered the room, fell on his knees on the mat, clasped his hands, and poured out a flood of passionate and somewhat hysterical extempore prayer, I should say at once and without the smallest hesitation, "Whatever else this man is, he is not an elderly and wealthy cleric of the Church of England. They don't do such things." Or suppose a man came to me pretending to be a qualified doctor, and flourished a stethoscope, or what he said was a stethoscope. I am glad to say that I have not even the remotest notion of what a stethoscope looks like; so that if he flourished a musical-box or a coffee-mill it would be all one to me. But I do think that I am not exaggerating my own sagacity if I say that I should begin to suspect the doctor if on entering my room he flung his legs and arms about, crying wildly, "Health! Health! priceless gift of Nature! I possess it! I overflow with it! I yearn to impart it! Oh, the sacred rapture of imparting health!" In that case I should suspect him of being rather in a position to receive than to offer medical superintendence.

Now, it is no exaggeration at all to say that any one who has ever known any soldiers (I can only answer for English and Irish and Scotch soldiers) would find it just as easy to believe that a real Bishop would grovel on the carpet in a religious ecstasy, or that a real doctor would dance about the drawing-room to show the invigorating effects of his own medicine, as to believe that a soldier, when asked for his authority, would point to a lot of shining weapons and declare symbolically that might was right. Of course, a real soldier would go rather red in the face and huskily repeat the proper formula, whatever it was, as that he came in the King's name.

Soldiers have many faults, but they have one redeeming merit; they are never worshippers of force. Soldiers more than any other men are taught severely and systematically that might is not right. The fact is obvious. The might is in the hundred men who obey. The right (or what is held to be right) is in the one man who commands them. They learn to obey symbols, arbitrary things, stripes on an arm, buttons on a coat, a title, a flag. These may be artificial things; they may be unreasonable things; they may, if you will, be wicked things; but they are weak things. They are not Force, and they do not look like Force. They are parts of an idea: of the idea of discipline; if you will, of the idea of tyranny; but still an idea. No soldier could possibly say that his own bayonets were his authority. No soldier could possibly say that he came in the name of his own bayonets. It would be as absurd as if a postman said that he came inside his bag. I do not, as I have said, underrate the evils that really do arise from militarism and the military ethic. It tends to give people wooden faces and sometimes wooden heads. It tends moreover (both through its specialisation and through its constant obedience) to a certain loss of real independence and strength of character. This has almost always been found when people made the mistake of turning the soldier into a statesman, under the mistaken impression that he was a strong man. The Duke of Wellington, for instance, was a strong soldier and therefore a weak statesman. But the soldier is always, by the nature of things, loyal to something. And as long as one is loyal to something one can never be a worshipper of mere force. For mere force, violence in the abstract, is the enemy of anything we love. To love anything is to see it at once under lowering skies of danger. Loyalty implies loyalty in misfortune; and when a soldier has accepted any nation's uniform he has already accepted its defeat.

Nevertheless, it does appear to be possible in Germany for a man to point to fixed bayonets and say, "These are my authority," and yet to convince ordinarily sane men that he is a soldier. If this is so, it does really seem to point to some habit of high-faultin' in the German nation, such as that of which I spoke previously. It almost looks as if the advisers, and even the officials, of the German Army had become infected in some degree with the false and feeble doctrine that might is right. As this doctrine is invariably preached by physical weaklings like Nietzsche it is a very serious thing even to entertain the supposition that it is affecting men who have really to do military work It would be the end of German soldiers to be affected by German philosophy. Energetic people use energy as a means, but only very tired people ever use energy as a reason. Athletes go in for games, because athletes desire glory. Invalids go in for calisthenics; for invalids (alone of all human beings) desire strength. So long as the German Army points to its heraldic eagle and says, "I come in the name of this fierce but fabulous animal," the German Army will be all right. If ever it says, "I come in the name of bayonets," the bayonets will break like glass, for only the weak exhibit strength without an aim.

At the same time, as I said before, do not let us forged our own faults. Do not let us forget them any the more easily because they are the opposite to the German faults. Modern England is too prone to present the spectacle of a person who is enormously delighted because he has not got the contrary disadvantages to his own. The Englishman is always saying "My house is not damp" at the moment when his house is on fire. The Englishman is always saying, "I have thrown off all traces of anæmia" in the middle of a fit of apoplexy. Let us always remember that if an Englishman wants to swindle English people, he does not dress up in the uniform of a soldier. If an Englishman wants to swindle English people he would as soon think of dressing up in the uniform of a messenger boy. Everything in England is done unofficially, casually, by conversations and cliques. The one Parliament that really does rule England is a secret Parliament; the debates of which must not be published—the Cabinet. The debates of the Commons are sometimes important; but only the debates in the Lobby, never the debates in the House. Journalists do control public opinion; but it is not controlled by the arguments they publish—it is controlled by the arguments between the editor and sub-editor, which they do not publish. This casualness is our English vice. It is at once casual and secret. Our public life is conducted privately. Hence it follows that if an English swindler wished to impress us, the last thing he would think of doing would be to put on a uniform. He would put on a polite slouching air and a careless, expensive suit of clothes; he would stroll up to the Mayor, be so awfully sorry to disturb him, find he had forgotten his card-case, mention, as if he were ashamed of it, that he was the Duke of Mercia, and carry the whole thing through with the air of a man who could get two hundred witnesses and two thousand retainers, but who was too tired to call any of them. And if he did it very well I strongly suspect that he would be as successful as the indefensible Captain at Koepenick.

Our tendency for many centuries past has been, not so much towards creating an aristocracy (which may or may not be a good thing in itself), as towards substituting an aristocracy for everything else. In England we have an aristocracy instead of a religion. The nobility are to the English poor what the saints and the fairies are to the Irish poor, what the large devil with a black face was to the

28

Scotch poor—the poetry of life. In the same way in England we have an aristocracy instead of a Government. We rely on a certain good humour and education in the upper class to interpret to us our contradictory Constitution. No educated man born of woman will be quite so absurd as the system that he has to administer. In short, we do not get good laws to restrain bad people. We get good people to restrain bad laws. And last of all we in England have an aristocracy instead of an Army. We have an Army of which the officers are proud of their families and ashamed of their uniforms. If I were a king of any country whatever, and one of my officers were ashamed of my uniform, I should be ashamed of my officer. Beware, then, of the really well-bred and apologetic gentleman whose clothes are at once quiet and fashionable, whose manner is at once diffident and frank. Beware how you admit him into your domestic secrets, for he may be a bogus Earl. Or, worse still, a real one.

THE BOY

I have no sympathy with international aggression when it is taken seriously, but I have a certain dark and wild sympathy with it when it is quite absurd. Raids are all wrong as practical politics, but they are human and imaginable as practical jokes. In fact, almost any act of ragging or violence can be forgiven on this strict condition—that it is of no use at all to anybody. If the aggressor gets anything out of it, then it is quite unpardonable. It is damned by the least hint of utility or profit. A man of spirit and breeding may brawl, but he does not steal. A gentleman knocks off his friend's hat; but he does not annex his friend's hat. For this reason (as Mr. Belloc has pointed out somewhere), the very militant French people have always returned after their immense raids—the raids of Godfrey the Crusader, the raids of Napoleon; "they are sucked back, having accomplished nothing but an epic."

Sometimes I see small fragments of information in the newspapers which make my heart leap with an irrational patriotic sympathy. I have had the misfortune to be left comparatively cold by many of the enterprises and proclamations of my country in recent times. But the other day I found in the *Tribune* the following paragraph, which I may be permitted to set down as an example of the kind of international outrage with which I have by far the most instinctive sympathy. There is something attractive, too, in the austere simplicity with which the affair is set forth—

"Geneva, Oct. 31.

"The English schoolboy Allen, who was arrested at Lausanne railway station on Saturday, for having painted red the statue of General Jomini of Payerne, was liberated yesterday, after paying a fine of £24. Allen has proceeded to Germany, where he will continue his studies. The people of Payerne are indignant, and clamoured for his detention in prison."

Now I have no doubt that ethics and social necessity require a contrary attitude, but I will freely confess that my first emotions on reading of this exploit were those of profound and elemental pleasure. There is something so large and simple about the operation of painting a whole stone General a bright red. Of course I can understand that the people of Payerne were indignant. They had passed to their homes at twilight through the streets of that beautiful city (or is it a province?), and they had seen against the silver ending of the sunset the grand grey figure of the hero of that land remaining to guard the town under the stars. It certainly must have been a shock to come out in the broad white morning and find a large vermilion General staring under the staring sun. I do not blame them at all for clamouring for the schoolboy's detention in prison; I dare say a little detention in prison would do him no harm. Still, I think the immense act has something about it human and excusable; and when I endeavour to analyse the reason of this feeling I find it to lie, not in the fact that the thing was big or bold or successful, but in the fact that the thing was perfectly useless to everybody, including the person who did it. The raid ends in itself; and so Master Allen is sucked back again, having accomplished nothing but an epic.

There is one thing which, in the presence of average modern journalism, is perhaps worth saying in connection with such an idle matter as this. The morals of a matter like this are exactly like the morals of anything else; they are concerned with mutual contract, or with the rights of independent human lives. But the whole modern world, or at any rate the whole modern Press, has a perpetual and consuming terror of plain morals. Men always attempt to avoid condemning a thing upon merely moral grounds. If I beat my grandmother to death to-morrow in the middle of Battersea Park, you may be perfectly certain that people will say everything about it except the simple and fairly obvious fact that it is wrong. Some will call it insane; that is, will accuse it of a deficiency of intelligence. This is not necessarily true at all. You could not tell whether the act was unintelligent or not unless you knew my grandmother. Some will call it vulgar, disgusting, and the rest of it; that is, they will accuse it of a lack of manners. Perhaps it does show a lack of manners; but this is scarcely its most serious disadvantage. Others will talk about the loathsome spectacle and the revolting scene; that is, they will accuse it of a deficiency of art, or æsthetic beauty. This again depends on the circumstances: in order to be quite certain that the appearance of the old lady has definitely deteriorated under the process of being beaten to death, it is necessary for the philosophical critic to be quite certain how ugly she was before. Another school of thinkers will say that the action is lacking in efficiency: that it is an uneconomic waste of a good grandmother. But that could only depend on the value, which is again an individual matter. The only real point that is worth mentioning is that the action is wicked, because your grandmother has a right not to be beaten to death. But of this simple moral explanation modern journalism has, as I say, a standing fear. It will call the action anything else—mad, bestial, vulgar, idiotic, rather than call it sinful.

One example can be found in such cases as that of the prank of the boy and the statue. When some trick of this sort is played, the newspapers opposed to it always describe it as "a senseless joke." What is the good of saying that? Every joke is a senseless joke. A joke is by its nature a protest against sense. It is no good attacking nonsense for being successfully nonsensical. Of course it is nonsensical to paint a celebrated Italian General a bright red; it is as nonsensical as "Alice in Wonderland." It is also, in my opinion, very nearly as funny. But the real answer to the affair is not to say that it is nonsensical or even to say that it is not funny, but to point out that it is wrong to spoil statues which belong to other people. If the modern world will not insist on having some sharp and definite moral law, capable of resisting the counter-attractions of art and humour, the modern world will simply be given over as a spoil to anybody who can manage to do a nasty thing in a nice way. Every murderer who can murder entertainingly will be allowed to murder. Every burglar who burgles in really humorous attitudes will burgle as much as he likes.

There is another case of the thing that I mean. Why on earth do the newspapers, in describing a dynamite outrage or any other political assassination, call it a "dastardly outrage" or a cowardly outrage? It is perfectly evident that it is not dastardly in the least. It is perfectly evident that it is about as cowardly as the Christians going to the lions. The man who does it exposes himself to the chance of being torn in pieces by two thousand people. What the thing is, is not cowardly, but profoundly and detestably wicked. The man who does it is very infamous and very brave. But, again, the explanation is that our modern Press would rather appeal to physical arrogance, or to anything, rather than appeal to right and wrong.

In most of the matters of modern England, the real difficulty is that there is a negative revolution without a positive revolution. Positive aristocracy is breaking up without any particular appearance of positive democracy taking its place. The polished class is becoming less polished without becoming less of a class; the nobleman who becomes a guinea-pig keeps all his privileges but loses some of his tradition; he becomes less of a gentleman without becoming less of a nobleman. In the same way (until some recent and happy revivals) it seemed highly probable that the Church of England would cease to be a religion long before it had ceased to be a Church. And in the same way, the vulgarisation of the old, simple middle class does not even have the advantage of doing away with class distinctions; the vulgar man is always the most distinguished, for the very desire to be distinguished is vulgar.

At the same time, it must be remembered that when a class has a morality it does not follow that it is an adequate morality. The middle-class ethic was inadequate for some purposes; so is the public-school ethic, the ethic of the upper classes. On this last matter of the public schools Dr. Spenser, the Head Master of University College School, has lately made some valuable observations. But even he, I think, overstates the claim of the public schools. "The strong point of the English public schools," he says, "has always lain in their efficiency as agencies for the formation of character and for the inculcation of the great notion of obligation which distinguishes a gentleman. On the physical and moral sides the public-school men of England are, I believe, unequalled." And he goes on to say that it is on the mental side that they are defective. But, as a matter of fact, the public-school training is in the strict sense defective upon the moral side also; it leaves out about half of morality. Its just claim is that, like the old middle class (and the Zulus), it trains some virtues and therefore suits some people for some situations. Put an old English merchant to serve in an army and he would have been irritated and clumsy. Put the men from English public schools to rule Ireland, and they make the greatest hash in human history.

Touching the morality of the public schools, I will take one point only, which is enough to prove the case. People have got into their heads an extraordinary idea that English public-school boys and English youth generally are taught to tell the truth. They are taught absolutely nothing of the kind. At no English public school is it even suggested, except by accident, that it is a man's duty to tell the truth. What is suggested is something entirely different: that it is a man's duty not to tell lies. So completely does this mistake soak through all civilisation that we hardly ever think even of the difference between the two things. When we say to a child, "You must tell the truth," we do merely mean that he must refrain from verbal inaccuracies. But the thing we never teach at all is the general duty of telling the truth, of giving a complete and fair picture of anything we are talking about, of not misrepresenting, not evading, not suppressing, not using plausible arguments that we know to be unfair, not selecting unscrupulously to prove an *ex parte* case, not telling all the nice stories about the Scotch, and all the nasty stories about the Irish, not pretending to be disinterested when you are really angry, not pretending to be angry when you are really only avaricious. The one thing that is never taught by any chance in the atmosphere of public schools is exactly that—that there is a whole truth of things, and that in knowing it and speaking it we are happy.

If any one has the smallest doubt of this neglect of truth in public schools he can kill his doubt with one plain question. Can any one on earth believe that if the seeing and telling of the whole truth were really one of the ideals of the English governing class, there could conceivably exist such a thing as the English party system? Why, the English party system is founded upon the principle that telling the whole truth does not matter. It is founded upon the principle that half a truth is better than no politics. Our system deliberately turns a crowd of men who might be impartial into irrational partisans. It teaches some of them to tell lies and all of them to believe lies. It gives every man an arbitrary brief that he has to work up as best he may and defend as best he can. It turns a room full of citizens into a room full of barristers. I know that it has many charms and virtues, fighting and good-fellowship; it has all the charms and virtues of a game. I only say that it would be a stark impossibility in a nation which believed in telling the truth.

LIMERICKS AND COUNSELS OF PERFECTION

It is customary to remark that modern problems cannot easily be attacked because they are so complex. In many cases I believe it is really because they are so simple. Nobody would believe in such simplicity of scoundrelism even if it were pointed out. People would say that the truth was a charge of mere melodramatic villainy; forgetting that nearly all villains really are melodramatic. Thus, for instance, we say that some good measures are frustrated or some bad officials kept in power by the press and confusion of public business; whereas very often the reason is simple healthy human bribery. And thus especially we say that the Yellow Press is exaggerative, over-emotional, illiterate, and anarchical, and a hundred other long words; whereas the only objection to it is that it tells lies. We waste our fine intellects in finding exquisite phraseology to fit a man, when in a well-ordered society we ought to be finding handcuffs to fit him.

This criticism of the modern type of righteous indignation must have come into many people's minds, I think, in reading Dr. Horton's eloquent expressions of disgust at the "corrupt Press," especially in connection with the Limerick craze. Upon the Limerick craze itself, I fear Dr. Horton will not have much effect; such fads perish before one has had time to kill them. But Dr. Horton's protest may really do good if it enables us to come to some clear understanding about what is really wrong with the popular Press, and which means it might be useful and which permissible to use for its reform. We do not want a censorship of the Press; but we are long past talking about that. At present it is not we that silence the Press; it is the Press that silences us. It is not a case of the Commonwealth settling how much the editors shall say; it is a case of the editors settling how much the Commonwealth shall know. If we attack the Press we shall be rebelling, not repressing. But shall we attack it?

Now it is just here that the chief difficulty occurs. It arises from the very rarity and rectitude of those minds which commonly inaugurate such crusades. I have the warmest respect for Dr. Horton's thirst after righteousness; but it has always seemed to me that his righteousness would be more effective without his refinement. The curse of the Nonconformists is their universal refinement. They dimly connect being good with being delicate, and even dapper; with not being grotesque or loud or violent; with not sitting down on one's hat. Now it is always a pleasure to be loud and violent, and sometimes it is a duty. Certainly it has nothing to do with sin; a man can be loudly and violently virtuous—nay, he can be loudly and violently saintly, though that is not the type of saintliness that we recognise in Dr. Horton. And as for sitting on one's hat, if it is done for any sublime object (as, for instance, to amuse the children), it is obviously an act of very beautiful self-sacrifice, the destruction and surrender of the symbol of personal dignity upon the shrine of public festivity. Now it will not do to attack the modern editor merely for being unrefined, like the great mass of mankind. We must be able to say that he is immoral, not that he is undignified or ridiculous. I do not mind the Yellow Press editor sitting on his hat. My only objection to him begins to dawn when he attempts to sit on my hat; or, indeed (as is at present the case), when he proceeds to sit on my head.

But in reading between the lines of Dr. Horton's invective one continually feels that he is not only angry with the popular Press for being unscrupulous: he is partly angry with the popular Press for being popular. He is not only irritated with Limericks for causing a mean money-scramble; he is also partly irritated with Limericks for being Limericks. The enormous size of the levity gets on his nerves, like the glare and blare of Bank Holiday. Now this is a motive which, however human and natural, must be strictly kept out of the way. It takes all sorts to make a world; and it is not in the least necessary that everybody should have that love of subtle and unobtrusive perfections in the matter of manners or literature which does often go with the type of the ethical idealist. It is not in the least desirable that everybody should be earnest. It is highly desirable that everybody should be honest, but that is a thing that can go quite easily with a coarse and cheerful character. But the ineffectualness of most protests against the abuse of the Press has been very largely due to the instinct

31

of democracy (and the instinct of democracy is like the instinct of one woman, wild but quite right) that the people who were trying to purify the Press were also trying to refine it; and to this the democracy very naturally and very justly objected. We are justified in enforcing good morals, for they belong to all mankind; but we are not justified in enforcing good manners, for good manners always mean our own manners. We have no right to purge the popular Press of all that we think vulgar or trivial. Dr. Horton may possibly loathe and detest Limericks just as I loathe and detest riddles; but I have no right to call them flippant and unprofitable; there are wild people in the world who like riddles. I am so afraid of this movement passing off into mere formless rhetoric and platform passion that I will even come close to the earth and lay down specifically some of the things that, in my opinion, could be, and ought to be, done to reform the Press.

First, I would make a law, if there is none such at present, by which an editor, proved to have published false news without reasonable verification, should simply go to prison. This is not a question of influences or atmospheres; the thing could be carried out as easily and as practically as the punishment of thieves and murderers. Of course there would be the usual statement that the guilt was that of a subordinate. Let the accused editor have the right of proving this if he can; if he does, let the subordinate be tried and go to prison. Two or three good rich editors and proprietors properly locked up would take the sting out of the Yellow Press better than centuries of Dr. Horton.

Second, it's impossible to pass over altogether the most unpleasant, but the most important part of this problem. I will deal with it as distantly as possible. I do not believe there is any harm whatever in reading about murders; rather, if anything, good; for the thought of death operates very powerfully with the poor in the creation of brotherhood and a sense of human dignity. I do not believe there is a pennyworth of harm in the police news, as such. Even divorce news, though contemptible enough, can really in most cases be left to the discretion of grown people; and how far children get hold of such things is a problem for the home and not for the nation. But there is a certain class of evils which a healthy man or woman can actually go through life without knowing anything about at all. These, I say, should be stamped and blackened out of every newspaper with the thickest black of the Russian censor. Such cases should either be always tried *in camera* or reporting them should be a punishable offence. The common weakness of Nature and the sins that flesh is heir to we can leave people to find in newspapers. Men can safely see in the papers what they have already seen in the streets. They may safely find in their journals what they have already found in themselves. But we do not want the imaginations of rational and decent people clouded with the horrors of some obscene insanity which has no more to do with human life than the man in Bedlam who thinks he is a chicken. And, if this vile matter is admitted, let it be simply with a mention of the Latin or legal name of the crime, and with no details whatever. As it is, exactly the reverse is true. Papers are permitted to terrify and darken the fancy of the young with innumerable details, but not permitted to state in clean legal language what the thing is about. They are allowed to give any fact about the thing except the fact that it is a sin.

Third, I would do my best to introduce everywhere the practice of signed articles. Those who urge the advantages of anonymity are either people who do not realise the special peril of our time or they are people who are profiting by it. It is true, but futile, for instance, to say that there is something noble in being nameless when a whole corporate body is bent on a consistent aim: as in an army or men building a cathedral. The point of modern newspapers is that there is no such corporate body and common aim; but each man can use the authority of the paper to further his own private fads and his own private finances.

ANONYMITY AND FURTHER COUNSELS

The end of the article which I write is always cut off, and, unfortunately, I belong to that lower class of animals in whom the tail is important. It is not anybody's fault but my own; it arises from the fact that I take such a long time to get to the point. Somebody, the other day, very reasonably complained of my being employed to write prefaces. He was perfectly right, for I always write a preface to the preface, and then I am stopped; also quite justifiably.

In my last article I said that I favoured three things—first, the legal punishment of deliberately false information; secondly, a distinction, in the matter of reported immorality, between those sins which any healthy man can see in himself and those which he had better not see anywhere; and thirdly, an absolute insistence in the great majority of cases upon the signing of articles. It was at this point that I was cut short, I will not say by the law of space, but rather by my own lawlessness in the matter of space. In any case, there is something more that ought to be said.

It would be an exaggeration to say that I hope some day to see an anonymous article counted as dishonourable as an anonymous letter. For some time to come, the idea of the leading article, expressing the policy of the whole paper, must necessarily remain legitimate; at any rate, we have all written such leading articles, and should never think the worse of any one for writing one. But I should certainly say that writing anonymously ought to have some definite excuse, such as that of the leading article. Writing anonymously ought to be the exception; writing a signed article ought to be the rule. And anonymity ought to be not only an exception, but an accidental exception; a man ought always to be ready to say what anonymous article he had written. The journalistic habit of counting it something sacred to keep secret the origin of an article is simply part of the conspiracy which seeks to put us who are journalists in the position of a much worse sort of Jesuits or Freemasons.

As has often been said, anonymity would be all very well if one could for a moment imagine that it was established from good motives. Suppose, for instance, that we were all quite certain that the men on the *Thunderer* newspaper were a band of brave young idealists who were so eager to overthrow Socialism, Municipal and National, that they did not care to which of them especially was given the glory of striking it down. Unfortunately, however, we do not believe this. What we believe, or, rather, what we know, is that the attack on Socialism in the *Thunderer* arises from a chaos of inconsistent and mostly evil motives, any one of which would lose simply by being named. A jerry-builder whose houses have been condemned writes anonymously and becomes the *Thunderer*. A Socialist who has quarrelled with the other Socialists writes anonymously, and he becomes the *Thunderer*. A monopolist who has lost his monopoly, and a demagogue who has lost his mob, can both write anonymously and become the same newspaper. It is quite true that there is a young and beautiful fanaticism in which men do not care to reveal their names. But there is a more elderly and a much more common excitement in which men do not dare to reveal them.

Then there is another rule for making journalism honest on which I should like to insist absolutely. I should like it to be a fixed thing that the name of the proprietor as well as the editor should be printed upon every paper. If the paper is owned by shareholders, let there be a list of shareholders. If (as is far more common in this singularly undemocratic age) it is owned by one man, let that one man's name be printed on the paper, if possible in large red letters. Then, if there are any obvious interests being served, we shall know that they are being served. My friends in Manchester are in a terrible state of excitement about the power of brewers and the dangers of admitting them to public office. But at least, if a man has controlled politics through beer, people generally know it: the subject of beer is too fascinating for any one to miss such personal peculiarities. But a man may control politics through journalism, and no ordinary English citizen know that he is controlling them at all. Again and again in the lists of Birthday Honours you and I have seen some Mr. Robinson suddenly elevated to the Peerage without any apparent reason. Even the Society papers (which we read with avidity) could tell us nothing about him except that he was a sportsman or a kind landlord, or interested in the breeding of badgers. Now I should like the name of that Mr. Robinson to be already familiar to the British public. I should like them to know already the public services for which they have to thank him. I should like them to have seen the name already on the outside of that organ of public opinion called *Tootsie's Tips*, or *The Boy Blackmailer*, or *Nosey Knows*, that bright little financial paper which did so much for the Empire and which so narrowly escaped a criminal prosecution. If they had seen it thus, they would estimate more truly and tenderly the full value of the statement in the Society paper that he is a true gentleman and a sound Churchman.

Finally, it should be practically imposed by custom (it so happens that it could not possibly be imposed by law) that letters of definite and practical complaint should be necessarily inserted by any editor in any paper. Editors have grown very much too lax in this respect. The old editor used dimly to regard himself as an unofficial public servant for the transmitting of public news. If he suppressed anything, he was supposed to have some special reason for doing so; as that the material was actually libellous or literally indecent. But the modern editor regards himself far too much as a kind of original artist, who can select and suppress facts with the arbitrary ease of a poet or a caricaturist. He "makes up" the paper as man "makes up" a fairy tale, he considers his newspaper solely as a work of art, meant to give pleasure, not to give news. He puts in this one letter because he thinks it clever. He puts in these three or four letters because he thinks them silly. He suppresses this article because he thinks it wrong. He suppresses this other and more dangerous article because he thinks it right. The old idea that he is simply a mode of the expression of the public, an "organ" of opinion, seems to have entirely vanished from his mind. To-day the editor is not only the organ, but the man who plays on the organ. For in all our modern movements we move away from Democracy.

This is the whole danger of our time. There is a difference between the oppression which has been too common in the past and the oppression which seems only too probable in the future. Oppression in the past, has commonly been an individual matter. The oppressors were as simple as the oppressed, and as lonely. The aristocrat sometimes hated his inferiors; he always hated his equals. The plutocrat was an individualist. But in our time even the plutocrat has become a Socialist. They have science and combination, and may easily inaugurate a much greater tyranny than the world has ever seen.

ON THE CRYPTIC AND THE ELLIPTIC

Surely the art of reporting speeches is in a strange state of degeneration. We should not object, perhaps, to the reporter's making the speeches much shorter than they are; but we do object to his making all the speeches much worse than they are. And the method which he employs is one which is dangerously unjust. When a statesman or philosopher makes an important speech, there are several courses which the reporter might take without being unreasonable. Perhaps the most reasonable course of all would be not to report the speech at all. Let the world live and love, marry and give in marriage, without that particular speech, as they did (in some desperate way) in the days when there were no newspapers. A second course would be to report a small part of it; but to get that right. A third course, far better if you can do it, is to understand the main purpose and argument of the speech, and report that in clear and logical language of your own. In short, the three possible methods are, first, to leave the man's speech alone; second, to report what he says or some complete part of what he says; and third, to report what he means. But the present way of reporting speeches (mainly created, I think, by the scrappy methods of the *Daily Mail*) is something utterly different from both these ways, and quite senseless and misleading.

The present method is this: the reporter sits listening to a tide of words which he does not try to understand, and does not, generally speaking, even try to take down; he waits until something occurs in the speech which for some reason sounds funny, or memorable, or very exaggerated, or, perhaps, merely concrete; then he writes it down and waits for the next one. If the orator says that the Premier is like a porpoise in the sea under some special circumstances, the reporter gets in the porpoise even if he leaves out the Premier. If the orator begins by saying that Mr. Chamberlain is rather like a violoncello, the reporter does not even wait to hear why he is like a violoncello. He has got hold of something material, and so he is quite happy. The strong words all are put in; the chain of thought is left out. If the orator uses the word "donkey," down goes the word "donkey." If the orator uses the word "damnable," down goes the word "damnable." They follow each other so abruptly in the report that it is often hard to discover the fascinating fact as to what was damnable or who was being compared with a donkey. And the whole line of argument in which these things occurred is entirely lost. I have before me a newspaper report of a speech by Mr. Bernard Shaw, of which one complete and separate paragraph runs like this—

"Capital meant spare money over and above one's needs. Their country was not really their country at all except in patriotic songs."

I am well enough acquainted with the whole map of Mr. Bernard Shaw's philosophy to know that those two statements might have been related to each other in a hundred ways. But I think that if they were read by an ordinary intelligent man, who happened not to know Mr. Shaw's views, he would form no impression at all except that Mr. Shaw was a lunatic of more than usually abrupt conversation and disconnected mind. The other two methods would certainly have done Mr. Shaw more justice: the reporter should either have taken down verbatim what the speaker really said about Capital, or have given an outline of the way in which this idea was connected with the idea about patriotic songs.

But we have not the advantage of knowing what Mr. Shaw really did say, so we had better illustrate the different methods from something that we do know. Most of us, I suppose, know Mark Antony's Funeral Speech in "Julius Cæsar." Now Mark Antony would have no reason to complain if he were not reported at all; if the *Daily Pilum* or the *Morning Fasces*, or whatever it was, confined itself to saying, "Mr. Mark Antony also spoke," or "Mr. Mark Antony, having addressed the audience, the meeting broke up in some confusion." The next honest method, worthy of a noble Roman reporter, would be that since he could not report the whole of the speech, he should report some of the speech. He might say—"Mr. Mark Antony, in the course of his speech, said—

' When that the poor have cried Cæsar hath wept:

Ambition should be made of sterner stuff."'

In that case one good, solid argument of Mark Antony would be correctly reported. The third and far higher course for the Roman reporter would be to give a philosophical statement of the purport of the speech. As thus—"Mr. Mark Antony, in the course of a powerful speech, conceded the high motives of the Republican leaders, and disclaimed any intention of raising the people against them; he thought, however, that many instances could be quoted against the theory of Cæsar's ambition, and he concluded by reading, at the request of the audience, the will of Cæsar, which proved that he had the most benevolent designs towards the Roman people." That is (I admit) not quite so fine as Shakspere, but it is a statement of the man's political position. But if a *Daily Mail* reporter were sent to take down Antony's oration, he would simply wait for any expressions that struck him as odd and put them down one after another without any logical connection at all. It would turn out something like this: "Mr. Mark Antony wished for his audience's ears. He had thrice offered Cæsar a crown. Cæsar was like a deer. If he were Brutus he would put a wound in every tongue. The stones of Rome would mutiny. See what a rent the envious Casca paid. Brutus was Cæsar's angel. The right honourable gentleman concluded by saying that he and the audience had all fallen down." That is the report of a political speech in a modern, progressive, or American manner, and I wonder whether the Romans would have put up with it.

The reports of the debates in the Houses of Parliament are constantly growing smaller and smaller in our newspapers. Perhaps this is partly because the speeches are growing duller and duller. I think in some degree the two things act and re-act on each other. For fear of the newspapers politicians are dull, and at last they are too dull even for the newspapers. The speeches in our time are more careful and elaborate, because they are meant to be read, and not to be heard. And exactly because they are more careful and elaborate, they are not so likely to be worthy of a careful and elaborate report. They are not interesting enough. So the moral cowardice of modern politicians has, after all, some punishment attached to it by the silent anger of heaven. Precisely because our political speeches are meant to be reported, they are not worth reporting. Precisely because they are carefully designed to be read, nobody reads them.

Thus we may concede that politicians have done something towards degrading journalism. It was not entirely done by us, the journalists. But most of it was. It was mostly the fruit of our first and most natural sin—the habit of regarding ourselves as conjurers rather than priests, for the definition is that a conjurer is apart from his audience, while a priest is a part of his. The conjurer despises his congregation; if the priest despises any one, it must be himself. The curse of all journalism, but especially of that yellow journalism which is the shame of our profession, is that we think ourselves cleverer than the people for whom we write, whereas, in fact, we are generally even stupider. But this insolence has its Nemesis; and that Nemesis is well illustrated in this matter of reporting.

For the journalist, having grown accustomed to talking down to the public, commonly talks too low at last, and becomes merely barbaric and unintelligible. By his very efforts to be obvious he becomes obscure. This just punishment may specially be noticed in the case of those staggering and staring headlines which American journalism introduced and which some English journalism imitates. I once saw a headline in a London paper which ran simply thus: "Dobbin's Little Mary." This was intended to be familiar and popular, and therefore, presumably, lucid. But it was some time before I realised, after reading about half the printed matter underneath, that it had something to do with the proper feeding of horses. At first sight, I took it, as the historical leader of the future will certainly take it, as containing some allusion to the little daughter who so monopolised the affections of the Major at the end of "Vanity Fair." The Americans carry to an even wilder extreme this darkness by excess of light. You may find a column in an American paper headed "Poet Brown Off Orange-flowers," or "Senator Robinson Shoehorns Hats Now," and it may be quite a long time before the full meaning breaks upon you: it has not broken upon me yet.

And something of this intellectual vengeance pursues also those who adopt the modern method of reporting speeches. They also become mystical, simply by trying to be vulgar. They also are condemned to be always trying to write like George R. Sims, and succeeding, in spite of themselves, in writing like Maeterlinck. That combination of words which I have quoted from an alleged speech of Mr. Bernard Shaw's was written down by the reporter with the idea that he was being particularly plain and democratic. But, as a matter of fact, if there is any connection between the two sentences, it must be something as dark as the deepest roots of Browning, or something as invisible as the most airy filaments of Meredith. To be simple and to be democratic are two very honourable and austere achievements; and it is not given to all the snobs and self-seekers to achieve them. High above even Maeterlinck or Meredith stand those, like Homer and Milton, whom no one can misunderstand. And Homer and Milton are not only better poets than Browning (great as he was), but they would also have been very much better journalists than the young men on the *Daily Mail.*

As it is, however, this misrepresentation of speeches is only a part of a vast journalistic misrepresentation of all life as it is. Journalism is popular, but it is popular mainly as fiction. Life is one world, and life seen in the newspapers another; the public enjoys both, but it is more or less conscious of the difference. People do not believe, for instance, that the debates in the House of Commons are as dramatic as they appear in the daily papers. If they did they would go, not to the daily paper, but to the House of Commons. The galleries would be crowded every night as they were in the French Revolution; for instead of seeing a printed story for a penny they would be seeing an acted drama for nothing. But the, people know in their hearts that journalism is a conventional art like any other, that it selects, heightens, and falsifies. Only its Nemesis is the same as that of other arts: if it loses all care for truth it loses all form likewise. The modern who paints too cleverly produces a picture of a cow which might be the earthquake at San Francisco. And the journalist who reports a speech too cleverly makes it mean nothing at all.

THE WORSHIP OF THE WEALTHY

There has crept, I notice, into our literature and journalism a new way of flattering the wealthy and the great. In more straightforward times flattery itself was more straight-forward; falsehood itself was more true. A poor man wishing to please a rich man simply said that he was the wisest, bravest, tallest, strongest, most benevolent and most beautiful of mankind; and as even the rich man probably knew that he wasn't that, the thing did the less harm. When courtiers sang the praises of a King they attributed to him things that were entirely improbable, as that he resembled the sun at noonday, that they had to shade their eyes when he entered the room, that his people could not breathe without him, or that he had with his single sword conquered Europe, Asia, Africa, and America. The safety of this method was its artificiality; between the King and his public image there was really no relation. But the moderns have invented a much subtler and more poisonous kind of eulogy. The modern method is to take the prince or rich man, to give a credible picture of his type of personality, as that he is business-like, or a sportsman, or fond of art, or convivial, or reserved; and then enormously exaggerate the value and importance of these natural qualities. Those who praise Mr. Carnegie do not say that he is as wise as Solomon and as brave as Mars; I wish they did. It would be the next most honest thing to giving their real reason for praising him, which is simply that he has money. The journalists who write about Mr. Pierpont Morgan do not say that he is as beautiful as Apollo; I wish they did. What they do is to take the rich man's superficial life and manner, clothes, hobbies, love of cats, dislike of doctors, or what not; and then with the assistance of this realism make the man out to be a prophet and a saviour of his kind, whereas he is merely a private and stupid man who happens to like cats or to dislike doctors. The old flatterer took for granted that the King was an ordinary man, and set to work to make him out extraordinary. The newer and cleverer flatterer takes for granted that he is extraordinary, and that therefore even ordinary things about him will be of interest.

I have noticed one very amusing way in which this is done. I notice the method applied to about six of the wealthiest men in England in a book of interviews published by an able and well-known journalist. The flatterer contrives to combine strict truth of fact with a vast atmosphere of awe and mystery by the simple operation of dealing almost entirely in negatives. Suppose you are writing a sympathetic study of Mr. Pierpont Morgan. Perhaps there is not much to say about what he does think, or like, or admire; but you can suggest whole vistas of his taste and philosophy by talking a great deal about what he does not think, or like, or admire. You say of him—"But little attracted to the most recent schools of German philosophy, he stands almost as resolutely aloof from the tendencies of transcendental Pantheism as from the narrower ecstasies of Neo-Catholicism." Or suppose I am called upon to praise the charwoman who has just come into my house, and who certainly deserves it much more. I say—"It would be a mistake to class Mrs. Higgs among the followers of Loisy; her position is in many ways different; nor is she wholly to be identified with the concrete Hebraism of Harnack." It is a splendid method, as it gives the flatterer an opportunity of talking about something else besides the subject of the flattery, and it gives the subject of the flattery a rich, if somewhat bewildered, mental glow, as of one who has somehow gone through agonies of philosophical choice of which he was previously unaware. It is a splendid method; but I wish it were applied sometimes to charwomen rather than only to millionaires.

There is another way of flattering important people which has become very common, I notice, among writers in the newspapers and elsewhere. It consists in applying to them the phrases "simple," or "quiet," or "modest," without any sort of meaning or relation to the person to whom they are applied. To be simple is the best thing in the world; to be modest is the next best thing. I am not so sure about being quiet. I am rather inclined to think that really modest people make a great deal of noise. It is quite self-evident that really simple people make a great deal of noise. But simplicity and modesty, at least, are very rare and royal human virtues, not to be lightly talked about. Few human beings, and at rare intervals, have really risen into being modest; not one man in ten or in twenty has by long wars become simple, as an actual old soldier does by [**Note: Apparent typesetting error here in original.] long wars become simple. These virtues are not things to fling about as mere flattery; many prophets and righteous men have desired to see these things and have not seen them. But in the description of the births, lives, and deaths of very luxurious men they are used incessantly and quite without thought. If a journalist has to describe a great politician or financier (the things are substantially the same) entering a room or walking down a thoroughfare, he always says, "Mr. Midas was quietly dressed in a black frock coat, a white waistcoat, and light grey trousers, with a plain green tie and simple flower in his button-hole." As if any one would expect him to have a crimson frock coat or spangled trousers. As if any one would expect him to have a burning Catherine wheel in his button-hole.

But this process, which is absurd enough when applied to the ordinary and external lives of worldly people, becomes perfectly intolerable when it is applied, as it always is applied, to the one episode which is serious even in the lives of politicians. I mean their death. When we have been sufficiently bored with the account of the simple costume of the millionaire, which is generally about as complicated as any that he could assume without being simply thought mad; when we have been told about the modest home of the millionaire, a home which is generally much too immodest to be called a home at all; when we have followed him through all these unmeaning eulogies, we are always asked last of all to admire his quiet funeral. I do not know what else people think a funeral should be except quiet. Yet again and again, over the grave of every one of those sad rich men, for whom one should surely feel, first and last, a speechless pity—over the grave of Beit, over the grave of Whiteley—this sickening nonsense about modesty and simplicity has been poured out. I well remember that when Beit was buried, the papers said that the mourning-coaches contained everybody of importance, that the floral tributes were sumptuous, splendid, intoxicating; but, for all that, it was a simple and quiet funeral. What, in the name of Acheron, did they expect it to be? Did they think there would be human sacrifice—the immolation of Oriental slaves upon the tomb? Did they think that long rows of Oriental dancing-girls would sway hither and thither in an ecstasy of lament? Did they look for the funeral games of Patroclus? I fear they had no such splendid and pagan meaning. I fear they were only using the words "quiet" and "modest" as words to fill up a page—a mere piece of the automatic hypocrisy which does become too common among those who have to write rapidly and often. The word "modest" will soon become like the word "honourable," which is said to be employed by the Japanese before any word that occurs in a polite sentence, as "Put honourable umbrella in honourable umbrella-stand;" or "condescend to clean honourable boots." We shall read in the future that the modest King went out in his modest crown, clad from head to foot in modest gold and attended with his ten thousand modest earls, their swords modestly drawn. No! if we have to pay for splendour let us praise it as splendour, not as simplicity. When next I meet a rich man I intend to walk up to him in the street and address him with Oriental hyperbole. He will probably run away.

SCIENCE AND RELIGION

In these days we are accused of attacking science because we want it to be scientific. Surely there is not any undue disrespect to our doctor in saying that he is our doctor, not our priest, or our wife, or ourself. It is not the business of the doctor to say that we must go to a watering-place; it is his affair to say that certain results of health will follow if we do go to a watering-place. After that, obviously, it is for us to judge. Physical science is like simple addition: it is either infallible or it is false. To mix science up with philosophy is only to produce a philosophy that has lost all its ideal value and a science that has lost all its practical value. I want my private physician to tell me whether this or that food will kill me. It is for my private philosopher to tell me whether I ought to be killed. I apologise for stating all these truisms. But the truth is, that I have just been reading a thick pamphlet written by a mass of highly intelligent men who seem never to have heard of any of these truisms in their lives.

Those who detest the harmless writer of this column are generally reduced (in their final ecstasy of anger) to calling him "brilliant;" which has long ago in our journalism become a mere expression of contempt. But I am afraid that even this disdainful phrase does me too much honour. I am more and more convinced that I suffer, not from a shiny or showy impertinence, but from a simplicity that verges upon imbecility. I think more and more that I must be very dull, and that everybody else in the modern world must be very clever. I have just been reading this important compilation, sent to me in the name of a number of men for whom I have a high respect, and called "New Theology and Applied Religion." And it is literally true that I have read through whole columns of the things without knowing what the people were talking about. Either they must be talking about some black and bestial religion in which they were brought up, and of which I never even heard, or else they must be talking about some blazing and blinding vision of God which they have found, which I have never found, and which by its very splendour confuses their logic and confounds their speech. But the best instance I can quote of the thing is in connection with this matter of the business of physical science on the earth, of which I have just spoken. The following words are written over the signature of a man whose intelligence I respect, and I cannot make head or tail of them—

"When modern science declared that the cosmic process knew nothing of a historical event corresponding to a Fall, but told, on the contrary, the story of an incessant rise in the scale of being, it was quite plain that the Pauline scheme—I mean the argumentative processes of Paul's scheme of salvation—had lost its very foundation; for was not that foundation the total depravity of the human race inherited from their first parents?.... But now there was no Fall; there was no total depravity, or imminent danger of endless doom; and, the basis gone, the superstructure followed."

It is written with earnestness and in excellent English; it must mean something. But what can it mean? How could physical science prove that man is not depraved? You do not cut a man open to find his sins. You do not boil him until he gives forth the unmistakable green fumes of depravity. How could physical science find any traces of a moral fall? What traces did the writer expect to find? Did he expect to find a fossil Eve with a fossil apple inside her? Did he suppose that the ages would have spared for him a complete skeleton of Adam attached to a slightly faded fig-leaf? The whole paragraph which I have quoted is simply a series of inconsequent sentences, all quite untrue in themselves and all quite irrelevant to each other. Science never said that there could have been no Fall. There might have been ten Falls, one on top of the other, and the thing would have been quite consistent with everything that we know from physical science. Humanity might have grown morally worse for millions of centuries, and the thing would in no way have contradicted the principle of Evolution. Men of science (not being raving lunatics) never said that there had been "an incessant

37

rise in the scale of being;" for an incessant rise would mean a rise without any relapse or failure; and physical evolution is full of relapse and failure. There were certainly some physical Falls; there may have been any number of moral Falls. So that, as I have said, I am honestly bewildered as to the meaning of such passages as this, in which the advanced person writes that because geologists know nothing about the Fall, therefore any doctrine of depravity is untrue. Because science has not found something which obviously it could not find, therefore something entirely different—the psychological sense of evil—is untrue. You might sum up this writer's argument abruptly, but accurately, in some way like this—"We have not dug up the bones of the Archangel Gabriel, who presumably had none, therefore little boys, left to themselves, will not be selfish." To me it is all wild and whirling; as if a man said—"The plumber can find nothing wrong with our piano; so I suppose that my wife does love me."

I am not going to enter here into the real doctrine of original sin, or into that probably false version of it which the New Theology writer calls the doctrine of depravity. But whatever else the worst doctrine of depravity may have been, it was a product of spiritual conviction; it had nothing to do with remote physical origins. Men thought mankind wicked because they felt wicked themselves. If a man feels wicked, I cannot see why he should suddenly feel good because somebody tells him that his ancestors once had tails. Man's primary purity and innocence may have dropped off with his tail, for all anybody knows. The only thing we all know about that primary purity and innocence is that we have not got it. Nothing can be, in the strictest sense of the word, more comic than to set so shadowy a thing as the conjectures made by the vaguer anthropologists about primitive man against so solid a thing as the human sense of sin. By its nature the evidence of Eden is something that one cannot find. By its nature the evidence of sin is something that one cannot help finding.

Some statements I disagree with; others I do not understand. If a man says, "I think the human race would be better if it abstained totally from fermented liquor," I quite understand what he means, and how his view could be defended. If a man says, "I wish to abolish beer because I am a temperance man," his remark conveys no meaning to my mind. It is like saying, "I wish to abolish roads because I am a moderate walker." If a man says, "I am not a Trinitarian," I understand. But if he says (as a lady once said to me), "I believe in the Holy Ghost in a spiritual sense," I go away dazed. In what other sense could one believe in the Holy Ghost? And I am sorry to say that this pamphlet of progressive religious views is full of baffling observations of that kind. What can people mean when they say that science has disturbed their view of sin? What sort of view of sin can they have had before science disturbed it? Did they think that it was something to eat? When people say that science has shaken their faith in immortality, what do they mean? Did they think that immortality was a gas?

Of course the real truth is that science has introduced no new principle into the matter at all. A man can be a Christian to the end of the world, for the simple reason that a man could have been an Atheist from the beginning of it. The materialism of things is on the face of things; it does not require any science to find it out. A man who has lived and loved falls down dead and the worms eat him. That is Materialism if you like. That is Atheism if you like. If mankind has believed in spite of that, it can believe in spite of anything. But why our human lot is made any more hopeless because we know the names of all the worms who eat him, or the names of all the parts of him that they eat, is to a thoughtful mind somewhat difficult to discover. My chief objection to these semi-scientific revolutionists is that they are not at all revolutionary. They are the party of platitude. They do not shake religion: rather religion seems to shake them. They can only answer the great paradox by repeating the truism.

THE METHUSELAHITE

I Saw in a newspaper paragraph the other day the following entertaining and deeply philosophical incident. A man was enlisting as a soldier at Portsmouth, and some form was put before him to be filled up, common, I suppose, to all such cases, in which was, among other things, an inquiry about what was his religion. With an equal and ceremonial gravity the man wrote down the word "Methuselahite." Whoever looks over such papers must, I should imagine, have seen some rum religions in his time; unless the Army is going to the dogs. But with all his specialist knowledge he could not "place" Methuselahism among what Bossuet called the variations of Protestantism. He felt a fervid curiosity about the tenets and tendencies of the sect; and he asked the soldier what it meant. The soldier replied that it was his religion "to live as long as he could."

Now, considered as an incident in the religious history of Europe, that answer of that soldier was worth more than a hundred cartloads of quarterly and monthly and weekly and daily papers discussing religious problems and religious books. Every day the daily paper reviews some new philosopher who has some new religion; and there is not in the whole two thousand words of the whole two columns one word as witty as or wise as that word "Methuselahite." The whole meaning of literature is simply to cut a long story short; that is why our modern books of philosophy are never literature. That soldier had in him the very soul of literature; he was one of the great phrase-makers of modern thought, like Victor Hugo or Disraeli. He found one word that defines the paganism of to-day.

Henceforward, when the modern philosophers come to me with their new religions (and there is always a kind of queue of them waiting all the way down the street) I shall anticipate their circumlocutions and be able to cut them short with a single inspired word. One of them will begin, "The New Religion, which is based upon that Primordial Energy in Nature...." "Methuselahite," I shall say sharply; "good morning." "Human Life," another will say, "Human Life, the only ultimate sanctity, freed from creed and dogma...." "Methuselahite!" I shall yell. "Out you go!" "My religion is the Religion of Joy," a third will explain (a bald old man with a cough and tinted glasses), "the Religion of Physical Pride and Rapture, and my...." "Methuselahite!" I shall cry again, and I shall slap him boisterously on the back, and he will fall down. Then a pale young poet with serpentine hair will come and say to me (as one did only the other day): "Moods and impressions are the only realities, and these are constantly and wholly changing. I could hardly therefore define my religion...." "I can," I should say, somewhat sternly. "Your religion is to live a long time; and if you stop here a moment longer you won't fulfil it."

A new philosophy generally means in practice the praise of some old vice. We have had the sophist who defends cruelty, and calls it masculinity. We have had the sophist who defends profligacy, and calls it the liberty of the emotions. We have had the sophist who defends idleness, and calls it art. It will almost certainly happen—it can almost certainly be prophesied—that in this saturnalia of sophistry there will at some time or other arise a sophist who desires to idealise cowardice. And when we are once in this unhealthy world of mere wild words, what a vast deal there would be to say for cowardice! "Is not life a lovely thing and worth saving?" the soldier would say as he ran away. "Should I not prolong the exquisite miracle of consciousness?" the householder would say as he hid under the table. "As long as there are roses and lilies on the earth shall I not remain here?" would come the voice of the citizen from under the bed. It would be quite easy to defend the coward as a kind of poet and mystic as it has been, in many recent books, to defend the emotionalist as a kind of poet and mystic, or the tyrant as a kind of poet and mystic. When that last grand sophistry and morbidity is preached in a book or on a platform, you may depend upon it there will be a great stir in its favour, that is, a great stir among the little people who live among books and platforms. There will be a new great Religion, the Religion of Methuselahism: with pomps and priests and altars. Its devout crusaders will vow themselves in thousands with a great vow to live long. But there is one comfort: they won't.

For, indeed, the weakness of this worship of mere natural life (which is a common enough creed to-day) is that it ignores the paradox of courage and fails in its own aim. As a matter of fact, no men would be killed quicker than the Methuselahites. The paradox of courage is that a man must be a little careless of his life even in order to keep it. And in the very case I have quoted we may see an example of how little the theory of Methuselahism really inspires our best life. For there is one riddle in that case which cannot easily be cleared up. If it was the man's religion to live as long as he could, why on earth was he enlisting as a soldier?

SPIRITUALISM.

I Have received a letter from a gentleman who is very indignant at what he considers my flippancy in disregarding or degrading Spiritualism. I thought I was defending Spiritualism; but I am rather used to being accused of mocking the thing that I set out to justify. My fate in most controversies is rather pathetic. It is an almost invariable rule that the man with whom I don't agree thinks I am making a fool of myself, and the man with whom I do agree thinks I am making a fool of him. There seems to be some sort of idea that you are not treating a subject properly if you eulogise it with fantastic terms or defend it by grotesque examples. Yet a truth is equally solemn whatever figure or example its exponent adopts. It is an equally awful truth that four and four make eight, whether you reckon the thing out in eight onions or eight angels, or eight bricks or eight bishops, or eight minor poets or eight pigs. Similarly, if it be true that God made all things, that grave fact can be asserted by pointing at a star or by waving an umbrella. But the case is stronger than this. There is a distinct philosophical advantage in using grotesque terms in a serious discussion.

I think seriously, on the whole, that the more serious is the discussion the more grotesque should be the terms. For this, as I say, there is an evident reason. For a subject is really solemn and important in so far as it applies to the whole cosmos, or to some great spheres and cycles of experience at least. So far as a thing is universal it is serious. And so far as a thing is universal it is full of comic things. If you take a small thing, it may be entirely serious: Napoleon, for instance, was a small thing, and he was serious: the same applies to microbes. If you isolate a thing, you may get the pure essence of gravity. But if you take a large thing (such as the Solar System) it *must* be comic, at least in parts. The germs are serious, because they kill you. But the stars are funny, because they give birth to life, and life gives birth to fun. If you have, let us say, a theory about man, and if you can only prove it by talking about Plato and George Washington, your theory may be a quite frivolous thing. But if you can prove it by talking about the butler or the postman, then it is serious, because it is universal. So far from it being irreverent to use silly metaphors on serious questions, it is one's duty to use silly metaphors on serious questions. It is the test of one's seriousness. It is the test of a responsible religion or theory whether it can take examples from pots and pans and boots and butter-tubs. It is the test of a good philosophy whether you can defend it grotesquely. It is the test of a good religion whether you can joke about it.

When I was a very young journalist I used to be irritated at a peculiar habit of printers, a habit which most persons of a tendency similar to mine have probably noticed also. It goes along with the fixed belief of printers that to be a Rationalist is the same thing as to be a Nationalist. I mean the printer's tendency to turn the word "cosmic" into the word "comic." It annoyed me at the time. But since then I have come to the conclusion that the printers were right. The democracy is always right. Whatever is cosmic is comic.

Moreover, there is another reason that makes it almost inevitable that we should defend grotesquely what we believe seriously. It is that all grotesqueness is itself intimately related to seriousness. Unless a thing is dignified, it cannot be undignified. Why is it funny that a man should sit down suddenly in the street? There is only one possible or intelligent reason: that man is the image of God. It is not funny that anything else should fall down; only that a man should fall down. No one sees anything funny in a tree falling down. No one sees a delicate absurdity in a stone falling down. No man stops in the road and roars with laughter at the sight of the snow coming down. The fall of thunderbolts is treated with some gravity. The fall of roofs and high buildings is taken seriously. It is only when a man tumbles down that we laugh. Why do we laugh? Because it is a grave religious matter: it is the Fall of Man. Only man can be absurd: for only man can be dignified.

The above, which occupies the great part of my article, is a parenthesis. It is time that I returned to my choleric correspondent who rebuked me for being too frivolous about the problem of Spiritualism. My correspondent, who is evidently an intelligent man, is very angry with me indeed. He uses the strongest language. He says I remind him of a brother of his: which seems to open an abyss or vista of infamy. The main substance of his attack resolves itself into two propositions. First, he asks me what right I have to talk about Spiritualism at all, as I admit I have never been to a *séance*. This is all very well, but there are a good many things to which I have never been, but I have not the smallest intention of leaving off talking about them. I refuse (for instance) to leave off talking about the Siege of Troy. I decline to be mute in the matter of the French Revolution. I will not be silenced on the late indefensible assassination of Julius Cæsar. If nobody has any right to judge of Spiritualism except a man who has been to a *séance*, the results, logically speaking, are rather serious: it would almost seem as if nobody had any right to judge of Christianity who had not been to the first meeting at Pentecost. Which would be dreadful. I conceive myself capable of forming my opinion of Spiritualism without seeing spirits, just as I form my opinion of the Japanese War without seeing the Japanese, or my opinion of American millionaires without (thank God) seeing an American millionaire. Blessed are they who have not seen and yet have believed: a passage which some have considered as a prophecy of modern journalism.

But my correspondent's second objection is more important. He charges me with actually ignoring the value of communication (if it exists) between this world and the next. I do not ignore it. But I do say this—That a different principle attaches to investigation in this spiritual field from investigation in any other. If a man baits a line for fish, the fish will come, even if he declares there are no such things as fishes. If a man limes a twig for birds, the birds will be caught, even if he thinks it superstitious to believe in birds at all. But a man cannot bait a line for souls. A man cannot lime a twig to catch gods. All wise schools have agreed that this latter capture depends to some extent on the faith of the capturer. So it comes to this: If you have no faith in the spirits your appeal is in vain; and if you have—is it needed? If you do not believe, you cannot. If you do—you will not.

That is the real distinction between investigation in this department and investigation in any other. The priest calls to the goddess, for the same reason that a man calls to his wife, because he knows she is there. If a man kept on shouting out very loud the single word "Maria," merely with the object of discovering whether if he did it long enough some woman of that name would come and marry him, he would be more or less in the position of the modern spiritualist. The old religionist cried out for his God. The new religionist cries out for some god to be his. The whole point of religion as it has hitherto existed in the world was that you knew all about your gods, even before you saw them, if indeed you ever did. Spiritualism seems to me absolutely right on all its mystical side. The supernatural part of it seems to me quite natural. The incredible part of it seems to me obviously true. But I think it so far dangerous or unsatisfactory that it is in some degree scientific. It inquires whether its gods are worth inquiring into. A man (of a certain age) may look into the eyes of his lady-love to see that they are beautiful. But no normal lady will allow that young man to look into her eyes to see whether they are beautiful. The same vanity and idiosyncrasy has been generally observed in gods. Praise them; or leave them alone; but do not look for them unless you know they are there. Do not look for them unless you want them. It annoys them very much.

THE ERROR OF IMPARTIALITY

The refusal of the jurors in the Thaw trial to come to an agreement is certainly a somewhat amusing sequel to the frenzied and even fantastic caution with which they were selected. Jurymen were set aside for reasons which seem to have only the very wildest relation to the case—reasons which we cannot conceive as giving any human being a real bias. It may be questioned whether the exaggerated theory of impartiality in an arbiter or juryman may not be carried so far as to be more unjust than partiality itself. What people call impartiality may simply mean indifference, and what people call partiality may simply mean mental activity. It is sometimes made an objection, for instance, to a juror that he has formed some *primâ-facie* opinion upon a case: if he can be forced under sharp questioning to admit that he has formed such an opinion, he is regarded as manifestly unfit to conduct the inquiry. Surely this is unsound. If his bias is one of interest, of class, or creed, or notorious propaganda, then that fact certainly proves that he is not an impartial arbiter. But the mere fact that he did form some temporary impression from the first facts as far as he knew them—this does not prove that he is not an impartial arbiter—it only proves that he is not a cold-blooded fool.

If we walk down the street, taking all the jurymen who have not formed opinions and leaving all the jurymen who have formed opinions, it seems highly probable that we shall only succeed in taking all the stupid jurymen and leaving all the thoughtful ones. Provided that the opinion formed is really of this airy and abstract kind, provided that it has no suggestion of settled motive or prejudice, we might well regard it not merely as a promise of capacity, but literally as a promise of justice. The man who took the trouble to deduce from the police reports would probably be the man who would take the trouble to deduce further and different things from the evidence. The man who had the sense to form an opinion would be the man who would have the sense to alter it.

It is worth while to dwell for a moment on this minor aspect of the matter because the error about impartiality and justice is by no means confined to a criminal question. In much more serious matters it is assumed that the agnostic is impartial; whereas the agnostic is merely ignorant. The logical outcome of the fastidiousness about the Thaw jurors would be that the case ought to be tried by Esquimaux, or Hottentots, or savages from the Cannibal Islands—by some class of people who could have no conceivable interest in the parties, and moreover, no conceivable interest in the case. The pure and starry perfection of impartiality would be reached by people who not only had no opinion before they had heard the case, but who also had no opinion after they had heard it. In the same way, there is in modern discussions of religion and philosophy an absurd assumption that a man is in some way just and well-poised because he has come to no conclusion; and that a man is in some way knocked off the list of fair judges because he has come to a conclusion. It is assumed that the sceptic has no bias; whereas he has a very obvious bias in favour of scepticism. I remember once arguing with an honest young atheist, who was very much shocked at my disputing some of the assumptions which were absolute sanctities to him (such as the quite unproved proposition of the independence of matter and the quite improbable proposition of its power to originate mind), and he at length fell back upon this question, which he delivered with an honourable heat of defiance and indignation: "Well, can you tell me any man of intellect, great in science or philosophy, who accepted the miraculous?" I said, "With pleasure. Descartes, Dr. Johnson, Newton, Faraday, Newman, Gladstone, Pasteur, Browning, Brunetiere—as many more as you please." To which that quite admirable and idealistic young man made this astonishing reply—"Oh, but of course they *had* to say that; they were Christians." First he challenged me to find a black swan, and then he ruled out all my swans because they were black. The fact that all these great intellects had come to the Christian view was somehow or other a proof either that they were not great intellects or that they had not really come to that view. The argument thus stood in a charmingly convenient form: "All men that count have come to my conclusion; for if they come to your conclusion they do not count."

It did not seem to occur to such controversialists that if Cardinal Newman was really a man of intellect, the fact that he adhered to dogmatic religion proved exactly as much as the fact that Professor Huxley, another man of intellect, found that he could not adhere to dogmatic religion; that is to say (as I cheerfully admit), it proved precious little either way. If there is one class of men whom history has proved especially and supremely capable of going quite wrong in all directions, it is the class of highly intellectual men. I would always prefer to go by the bulk of humanity; that is why I am a democrat. But whatever be the truth about exceptional intelligence and the masses, it is manifestly most unreasonable that intelligent men should be divided upon the absurd modern principle of regarding every clever man who cannot make up his mind as an impartial judge, and regarding every clever man who can make up his mind as a servile fanatic. As it is, we seem to regard it as a positive objection to a reasoner that he has taken one side or the other. We regard it (in other words) as a positive objection to a reasoner that he has contrived to reach the object of his reasoning. We call a man a bigot or a slave of dogma because he is a thinker who has thought thoroughly and to a definite end. We say that the juryman is not a juryman because he has brought in a verdict. We

41

say that the judge is not a judge because he gives judgment. We say that the sincere believer has no right to vote, simply because he has voted.

PHONETIC SPELLING

A correspondent asks me to make more lucid my remarks about phonetic spelling. I have no detailed objection to items of spelling-reform; my objection is to a general principle; and it is this. It seems to me that what is really wrong with all modern and highly civilised language is that it does so largely consist of dead words. Half our speech consists of similes that remind us of no similarity; of pictorial phrases that call up no picture; of historical allusions the origin of which we have forgotten. Take any instance on which the eye happens to alight. I saw in the paper some days ago that the well-known leader of a certain religious party wrote to a supporter of his the following curious words: "I have not forgotten the talented way in which you held up the banner at Birkenhead." Taking the ordinary vague meaning of the word "talented," there is no coherency in the picture. The trumpets blow, the spears shake and glitter, and in the thick of the purple battle there stands a gentleman holding up a banner in a talented way. And when we come to the original force of the word "talent" the matter is worse: a talent is a Greek coin used in the New Testament as a symbol of the mental capital committed to an individual at birth. If the religious leader in question had really meant anything by his phrases, he would have been puzzled to know how a man could use a Greek coin to hold up a banner. But really he meant nothing by his phrases. "Holding up the banner" was to him a colourless term for doing the proper thing, and "talented" was a colourless term for doing it successfully.

Now my own fear touching anything in the way of phonetic spelling is that it would simply increase this tendency to use words as counters and not as coins. The original life in a word (as in the word "talent") burns low as it is: sensible spelling might extinguish it altogether. Suppose any sentence you like: suppose a man says, "Republics generally encourage holidays." It looks like the top line of a copy-book. Now, it is perfectly true that if you wrote that sentence exactly as it is pronounced, even by highly educated people, the sentence would run: "Ripubliks jenrally inkurrij hollidies." It looks ugly: but I have not the smallest objection to ugliness. My objection is that these four words have each a history and hidden treasures in them: that this history and hidden treasure (which we tend to forget too much as it is) phonetic spelling tends to make us forget altogether. Republic does not mean merely a mode of political choice. Republic (as we see when we look at the structure of the word) means the Public Thing: the abstraction which is us all.

A Republican is not a man who wants a Constitution with a President. A Republican is a man who prefers to think of Government as impersonal; he is opposed to the Royalist, who prefers to think of Government as personal. Take the second word, "generally." This is always used as meaning "in the majority of cases." But, again, if we look at the shape and spelling of the word, we shall see that "generally" means something more like "generically," and is akin to such words as "generation" or "regenerate." "Pigs are generally dirty" does not mean that pigs are, in the majority of cases, dirty, but that pigs as a race or genus are dirty, that pigs as pigs are dirty—an important philosophical distinction. Take the third word, "encourage." The word "encourage" is used in such modern sentences in the merely automatic sense of promote; to encourage poetry means merely to advance or assist poetry. But to encourage poetry means properly to put courage into poetry—a fine idea. Take the fourth word, "holidays." As long as that word remains, it will always answer the ignorant slander which asserts that religion was opposed to human cheerfulness; that word will always assert that when a day is holy it should also be happy. Properly spelt, these words all tell a sublime story, like Westminster Abbey. Phonetically spelt, they might lose the last traces of any such story. "Generally" is an exalted metaphysical term; "jenrally" is not. If you "encourage" a man, you pour into him the chivalry of a hundred princes; this does not happen if you merely "inkurrij" him. "Republics," if spelt phonetically, might actually forget to be public. "Holidays," if spelt phonetically, might actually forget to be holy.

Here is a case that has just occurred. A certain magistrate told somebody whom he was examining in court that he or she "should always be polite to the police." I do not know whether the magistrate noticed the circumstance, but the word "polite" and the word "police" have the same origin and meaning. Politeness means the atmosphere and ritual of the city, the symbol of human civilisation. The policeman means the representative and guardian of the city, the symbol of human civilisation. Yet it may be doubted whether the two ideas are commonly connected in the mind. It is probable that we often hear of politeness without thinking of a policeman; it is even possible that our eyes often alight upon a policeman without our thoughts instantly flying to the subject of politeness. Yet the idea of the sacred city is not only the link of them both, it is the only serious justification and the only serious corrective of them both. If politeness means too often a mere frippery, it is because it has not enough to do with serious patriotism and public dignity; if policemen are coarse or casual, it is because they are not sufficiently convinced that they are the servants of the beautiful city and the

42

agents of sweetness and light. Politeness is not really a frippery. Politeness is not really even a thing merely suave and deprecating. Politeness is an armed guard, stern and splendid and vigilant, watching over all the ways of men; in other words, politeness is a policeman. A policeman is not merely a heavy man with a truncheon: a policeman is a machine for the smoothing and sweetening of the accidents of everyday existence. In other words, a policeman is politeness; a veiled image of politeness—sometimes impenetrably veiled. But my point is here that by losing the original idea of the city, which is the force and youth of both the words, both the things actually degenerate. Our politeness loses all manliness because we forget that politeness is only the Greek for patriotism. Our policemen lose all delicacy because we forget that a policeman is only the Greek for something civilised. A policeman should often have the functions of a knight-errant. A policeman should always have the elegance of a knight-errant. But I am not sure that he would succeed any the better n remembering this obligation of romantic grace if his name were spelt phonetically, supposing that it could be spelt phonetically. Some spelling-reformers, I am told, in the poorer parts of London do spell his name phonetically, very phonetically. They call him a "pleeceman." Thus the whole romance of the ancient city disappears from the word, and the policeman's reverent courtesy of demeanour deserts him quite suddenly. This does seem to me the case against any extreme revolution in spelling. If you spell a word wrong you have some temptation to think it wrong.

HUMANITARIANISM AND STRENGTH

Somebody writes complaining of something I said about progress. I have forgotten what I said, but I am quite certain that it was (like a certain Mr. Douglas in a poem which I have also forgotten) tender and true. In any case, what I say now is this. Human history is so rich and complicated that you can make out a case for any course of improvement or retrogression. I could make out that the world has been growing more democratic, for the English franchise has certainly grown more democratic. I could also make out that the world has been growing more aristocratic, for the English Public Schools have certainly grown more aristocratic I could prove the decline of militarism by the decline of flogging; I could prove the increase of militarism by the increase of standing armies and conscription. But I can prove anything in this way. I can prove that the world has always been growing greener. Only lately men have invented absinthe and the *Westminster Gazette*. I could prove the world has grown less green. There are no more Robin Hood foresters, and fields are being covered with houses. I could show that the world was less red with khaki or more red with the new penny stamps. But in all cases progress means progress only in some particular thing. Have you ever noticed that strange line of Tennyson, in which he confesses, half consciously, how very *conventional* progress is?—

"Let the great world spin for ever down the ringing

grooves of change."

Even in praising change, he takes for a simile the most unchanging thing. He calls our modern change a groove. And it is a groove; perhaps there was never anything so groovy.

Nothing would induce me in so idle a monologue as this to discuss adequately a great political matter like the question of the military punishments in Egypt. But I may suggest one broad reality to be observed by both sides, and which is, generally speaking, observed by neither. Whatever else is right, it is utterly wrong to employ the argument that we Europeans must do to savages and Asiatics whatever savages and Asiatics do to us. I have even seen some controversialists use the metaphor, "We must fight them with their own weapons." Very well; let those controversialists take their metaphor, and take it literally. Let us fight the Soudanese with their own weapons. Their own weapons are large, very clumsy knives, with an occasional old-fashioned gun. Their own weapons are also torture and slavery. If we fight them with torture and slavery, we shall be fighting badly, precisely as if we fought them with clumsy knives and old guns. That is the whole strength of our Christian civilisation, that it does fight with its own weapons and not with other people's. It is not true that superiority suggests a tit for tat. It is not true that if a small hooligan puts his tongue out at the Lord Chief Justice, the Lord Chief Justice immediately realises that his only chance of maintaining his position is to put his tongue out at the little hooligan. The hooligan may or may not have any respect at all for the Lord Chief Justice: that is a matter which we may contentedly leave as a solemn psychological mystery. But if the hooligan has any respect at all for the Lord Chief Justice, that respect is certainly extended to the Lord Chief Justice entirely because he does not put his tongue out.

Exactly in the same way the ruder or more sluggish races regard the civilisation of Christendom. If they have any respect for it, it is precisely because it does not use their own coarse and cruel expedients. According to some modern moralists whenever Zulus cut off the heads of dead Englishmen, Englishmen must cut off the heads of dead Zulus. Whenever Arabs or Egyptians constantly use the whip to their slaves, Englishmen must use the whip to their subjects. And on a similar principle (I suppose), whenever an English Admiral has to fight cannibals the English Admiral ought to eat them. However unattractive a menu consisting entirely of barbaric kings may appear to an English gentleman, he must try to sit down to it with an appetite. He must fight the Sandwich Islanders with their own weapons; and their own weapons are knives and forks. But the truth of the matter is, of course, that to do this kind of thing is to break the whole spell of our supremacy. All the mystery of the white man, all the fearful poetry of the white man, so far as it exists in the eyes of these savages, consists in the fact that we do not do such things. The Zulus point at us and say, "Observe the advent of these inexplicable demi-gods, these magicians, who do not cut off the noses of their enemies." The Soudanese say to each other, "This hardy people never flogs its servants; it is superior to the simplest and most obvious human pleasures." And the cannibals say, "The austere and terrible race, the race that denies itself even boiled missionary, is upon us: let us flee."

Whether or no[** "not"? or just his style?] these details are a little conjectural, the general proposition I suggest is the plainest common sense. The elements that make Europe upon the whole the most humanitarian civilisation are precisely the elements that make it upon the whole the strongest. For the power which makes a man able to entertain a good impulse is the same as that which enables him to make a good gun; it is imagination. It is imagination that makes a man outwit his enemy, and it is imagination that makes him spare his enemy. It is precisely because this picturing of the other man's point of view is in the main a thing in which Christians and Europeans specialise that Christians and Europeans, with all their faults, have carried to such perfection both the arts of peace and war.

They alone have invented machine-guns, and they alone have invented ambulances; they have invented ambulances (strange as it may sound) for the same reason for which they have invented machine-guns. Both involve a vivid calculation of remote events. It is precisely because the East, with all its wisdom, is cruel, that the East, with all its wisdom, is weak. And it is precisely because savages are pitiless that they are still—merely savages. If they could imagine their enemy's sufferings they could also imagine his tactics. If Zulus did not cut off the Englishman's head they might really borrow it. For if you do not understand a man you cannot crush him. And if you do understand him, very probably you will not.

When I was about seven years old I used to think that the chief modern danger was a danger of over-civilisation. I am inclined to think now that the chief modern danger is that of a slow return towards barbarism, just such a return towards barbarism as is indicated in the suggestions of barbaric retaliation of which I have just spoken. Civilisation in the best sense merely means the full authority of the human spirit over all externals. Barbarism means the worship of those externals in their crude and unconquered state. Barbarism means the worship of Nature; and in recent poetry, science, and philosophy there has been too much of the worship of Nature. Wherever men begin to talk much and with great solemnity about the forces outside man, the note of it is barbaric. When men talk much about heredity and environment they are almost barbarians. The modern men of science are many of them almost barbarians. Mr. Blatchford is in great danger of becoming a barbarian. For barbarians (especially the truly squalid and unhappy barbarians) are always talking about these scientific subjects from morning till night. That is why they remain squalid and unhappy; that is why they remain barbarians. Hottentots are always talking about heredity, like Mr. Blatchford. Sandwich Islanders are always talking about environment, like Mr. Suthers. Savages—those that are truly stunted or depraved—dedicate nearly all their tales and sayings to the subject of physical kinship, of a curse on this or that tribe, of a taint in this or that family, of the invincible law of blood, of the unavoidable evil of places. The true savage is a slave, and is always talking about what he must do; the true civilised man is a free man and is always talking about what he may do. Hence all the Zola heredity and Ibsen heredity that has been written in our time affects me as not merely evil, but as essentially ignorant and retrogressive. This sort of science is almost the only thing that can with strict propriety be called reactionary. Scientific determinism is simply the primal twilight of all mankind; and some men seem to be returning to it.

Another savage trait of our time is the disposition to talk about material substances instead of about ideas. The old civilisation talked about the sin of gluttony or excess. We talk about the Problem of Drink—as if drink could be a problem. When people have come to call the problem of human intemperance the Problem of Drink, and to talk about curing it by attacking the drink traffic, they have reached quite a dim stage of barbarism. The thing is an inverted form of fetish worship; it is no sillier to say that a bottle is a god than to say that a bottle is a devil. The people who talk about the curse of drink will probably progress down that dark hill. In a little while we shall have them calling the practice of wife-beating the Problem of Pokers; the habit of housebreaking will be called the Problem of the Skeleton-Key Trade; and for all I know they may try to prevent forgery by shutting up all the stationers' shops by Act of Parliament.

I cannot help thinking that there is some shadow of this uncivilised materialism lying at present upon a much more dignified and valuable cause. Every one is talking just now about the desirability of ingeminating peace and averting war. But even war and peace are physical states rather than moral states, and in talking about them only we have by no means got to the bottom of the matter. How, for instance, do we as a matter of fact create peace in one single community? We do not do it by vaguely telling every one to avoid fighting and to submit to anything that is done to him. We do it by definitely defining his rights and then undertaking to avenge his wrongs. We shall never have a common peace in Europe till we have a common principle in Europe. People talk of "The United States of Europe;" but they forget that it needed the very doctrinal "Declaration of Independence" to make the United States of America. You cannot agree about nothing any more than you can quarrel about nothing.

WINE WHEN IT IS RED

I suppose that there will be some wigs on the green in connection with the recent manifesto signed by a string of very eminent doctors on the subject of what is called "alcohol." "Alcohol" is, to judge by the sound of it, an Arabic word, like "algebra" and "Alhambra," those two other unpleasant things. The Alhambra in Spain I have never seen; I am told that it is a low and rambling building; I allude to the far more dignified erection in Leicester Square. If it is true, as I surmise, that "alcohol" is a word of the Arabs, it is interesting to realise that our general word for the essence of wine and beer and such things comes from a people which has made particular war upon them. I suppose that some aged Moslem chieftain sat one day at the opening of his tent and, brooding with black brows and cursing in his black beard over wine as the symbol of Christianity, racked his brains for some word ugly enough to express his racial and religious antipathy, and suddenly spat out the horrible word "alcohol." The fact that the doctors had to use this word for the sake of scientific clearness was really a great disadvantage to them in fairly discussing the matter. For the word really involves one of those beggings of the question which make these moral matters so difficult. It is quite a mistake to suppose that, when a man desires an alcoholic drink, he necessarily desires alcohol.

Let a man walk ten miles steadily on a hot summer's day along a dusty English road, and he will soon discover why beer was invented. The fact that beer has a very slight stimulating quality will be quite among the smallest reasons that induce him to ask for it. In short, he will not be in the least desiring alcohol; he will be desiring beer. But, of course, the question cannot be settled in such a simple way. The real difficulty which confronts everybody, and which especially confronts doctors, is that the extraordinary position of man in the physical universe makes it practically impossible to treat him in either one direction or the other in a purely physical way. Man is an exception, whatever else he is. If he is not the image of God, then he is a disease of the dust. If it is not true that a divine being fell, then we can only say that one of the animals went entirely off its head. In neither case can we really argue very much from the body of man simply considered as the body of an innocent and healthy animal. His body has got too much mixed up with his soul, as we see in the supreme instance of sex. It may be worth while uttering the warning to wealthy philanthropists and idealists that this argument from the animal should not be thoughtlessly used, even against the atrocious evils of excess; it is an argument that proves too little or too much.

Doubtless, it is unnatural to be drunk. But then in a real sense it is unnatural to be human. Doubtless, the intemperate workman wastes his tissues in drinking; but no one knows how much the sober workman wastes his tissues by working. No one knows how much the wealthy philanthropist wastes his tissues by talking; or, in much rarer conditions, by thinking. All the human things are more dangerous than anything that affects the beasts—sex, poetry, property, religion. The real case against drunkenness is not that it calls up the beast, but that it calls up the Devil. It does not call up the beast, and if it did it would not matter much, as a rule; the beast is a harmless and rather amiable creature, as anybody can see by watching cattle. There is nothing bestial about intoxication; and certainly there is nothing intoxicating or even particularly lively about beasts. Man is always something worse or something better than an animal; and a mere argument from animal perfection never touches him at all. Thus, in sex no animal is either chivalrous or obscene. And thus no animal ever invented anything so bad as drunkenness—or so good as drink.

The pronouncement of these particular doctors is very clear and uncompromising; in the modern atmosphere, indeed, it even deserves some credit for moral courage. The majority of modern people, of course, will probably agree with it in so far as it declares that alcoholic drinks are often of supreme value in emergencies of illness; but many people, I fear, will open their eyes at the emphatic terms in which they describe such drink as considered as a beverage; but they are not content with declaring that the drink is in moderation harmless: they distinctly declare that it is in moderation beneficial. But I fancy that, in saying this, the doctors had in mind a truth that runs somewhat counter to the common opinion. I fancy that it is the experience of most doctors that giving any alcohol for illness (though often necessary) is about the most morally dangerous way of giving it. Instead of giving it to a healthy person who has many other forms of life, you are giving it to a desperate person, to whom it is the only form of life. The invalid can hardly be blamed if by some accident of his erratic and overwrought condition he comes to remember the thing as the very water of vitality and to use it as such. For in so far as drinking is really a sin it is not because drinking is wild, but because drinking is tame; not in so far as it is anarchy, but in so far as it is slavery. Probably the worst way to drink is to drink medicinally. Certainly the safest way to drink is to drink carelessly; that is, without caring much for anything, and especially not caring for the drink.

The doctor, of course, ought to be able to do a great deal in the way of restraining those individual cases where there is plainly an evil thirst; and beyond that the only hope would seem to be in some increase, or, rather, some concentration of ordinary public opinion on the subject. I have always held consistently my own modest theory on the subject. I believe that if by some method the local public-house could be as definite and isolated a place as the local post-office or the local railway station, if all types of people passed through it for all types of refreshment, you would have the same safeguard against a man behaving in a disgusting way in a tavern that you have at present against his behaving in a disgusting way in a post-office: simply the presence of his ordinary sensible neighbours. In such a place the kind of lunatic who wants to drink an unlimited number of whiskies would be treated with the same severity with which the post office authorities would treat an amiable lunatic who had an appetite for licking an unlimited number of stamps. It is a small matter whether in either case a technical refusal would be officially employed. It is an essential matter that in both cases the authorities could rapidly communicate with the friends and family of the mentally afflicted person. At least, the postmistress would not dangle a strip of tempting sixpenny stamps before the enthusiast's eyes as he was being dragged away with his tongue out. If we made drinking open and official we might be taking one step towards making it careless. In such things to be careless is to be sane: for neither drunkards nor Moslems can be careless about drink.

I once heard a man call this age the age of demagogues. Of this I can only say, in the admirably sensible words of the angry coachman in "Pickwick," that "that remark's political, or what is much the same, it ain't true." So far from being the age of demagogues, this is really and specially the age of mystagogues. So far from this being a time in which things are praised because they are popular, the truth is that this is the first time, perhaps, in the whole history of the world in which things can be praised because they are unpopular. The demagogue succeeds because he makes himself understood, even if he is not worth understanding. But the mystagogue succeeds because he gets himself misunderstood; although, as a rule, he is not even worth misunderstanding. Gladstone was a demagogue: Disraeli a mystagogue. But ours is specially the time when a man can advertise his wares not as a universality, but as what the tradesmen call "a speciality." We all know this, for instance, about modern art. Michelangelo and Whistler were both fine artists; but one is obviously public, the other obviously private, or, rather, not obvious at all. Michelangelo's frescoes are doubtless finer than the popular judgment, but they are plainly meant to strike the popular judgment. Whistler's pictures seem often meant to escape the popular judgment; they even seem meant to escape the popular admiration. They are elusive, fugitive; they fly even from praise. Doubtless many artists in Michelangelo's day declared themselves to be great artists, although they were unsuccessful. But they did not declare themselves great artists because they were unsuccessful: that is the peculiarity of our own time, which has a positive bias against the populace.

Another case of the same kind of thing can be found in the latest conceptions of humour. By the wholesome tradition of mankind, a joke was a thing meant to amuse men; a joke which did not amuse them was a failure, just as a fire which did not warm them was a failure. But we have seen the process of secrecy and aristocracy introduced even into jokes. If a joke falls flat, a small school of æsthetes only ask us to notice the wild grace of its falling and its perfect flatness after its fall. The old idea that the joke was not good enough for the company has been superseded by the new aristocratic idea that the company was not worthy of the joke. They have introduced an almost insane individualism into that one form of intercourse which is specially and uproariously communal. They have made even levities into secrets. They have made laughter lonelier than tears.

There is a third thing to which the mystagogues have recently been applying the methods of a secret society: I mean manners. Men who sought to rebuke rudeness used to represent manners as reasonable and ordinary; now they seek to represent them as private and peculiar. Instead of saying to a man who blocks up a street or the fireplace, "You ought to know better than that," the moderns say, "You, of course, don't know better than that."

I have just been reading an amusing book by Lady Grove called "The Social Fetich," which is a positive riot of this new specialism and mystification. It is due to Lady Grove to say that she has some of the freer and more honourable qualities of the old Whig aristocracy, as well as their wonderful worldliness and their strange faith in the passing fashion of our politics. For instance, she speaks of Jingo Imperialism with a healthy English contempt; and she perceives stray and striking truths, and records them justly—as, for instance, the greater democracy of the Southern and Catholic countries of Europe. But in her dealings with social formulæ here in England she is, it must frankly be said, a common mystagogue. She does not, like a decent demagogue, wish to make people understand; she wishes to make them painfully conscious of not understanding. Her favourite method is to terrify people from doing things that are quite harmless by telling them that if they do they are the kind of people who would do other things, equally harmless. If you ask after somebody's mother (or whatever it is), you are the kind of person who would have a pillow-case, or would not have a pillow-case. I forget which it is; and so, I dare say, does she. If you assume the ordinary dignity of a decent citizen and say that you don't see the harm of having a mother or a pillow-case, she would say that of course _you_ wouldn't. This is what I call being a mystagogue. It is more vulgar than being a demagogue; because it is much easier.

The primary point I meant to emphasise is that this sort of aristocracy is essentially a new sort. All the old despots were demagogues; at least, they were demagogues whenever they were really trying to please or impress the demos. If they poured out beer for their vassals it was because both they and their vassals had a taste for beer. If (in some slightly different mood) they poured melted lead on their vassals, it was because both they and their vassals had a strong distaste for melted lead. But they did not make any mystery about either of the two substances. They did not say, "You don't like melted lead?.... Ah! no, of course, _you_ wouldn't; you are probably the kind of person who would prefer beer.... It is no good asking you even to imagine the curious undercurrent of psychological pleasure felt by a refined person under the seeming shock of melted lead." Even tyrants when they tried to be popular, tried to give the people pleasure; they did not try to overawe the people by giving them something which they ought to regard as pleasure. It was the same with the popular presentment of aristocracy. Aristocrats tried to impress humanity by the exhibition of qualities which humanity admires, such as courage, gaiety, or even mere splendour. The aristocracy might have more possession in these things, but the democracy had quite equal delight in them. It was much more sensible to offer yourself for admiration because you had drunk three bottles of port at a sitting, than to offer yourself for admiration (as Lady Grove does) because you think it right to say "port wine" while other people think it right to say "port." Whether Lady Grove's preference for port wine (I mean for the phrase port wine) is a piece of mere nonsense I do not know; but at least it is a very good example of the futility of such tests in the matter even of mere breeding. "Port wine" may happen to be the phrase used in certain good families; but numberless aristocrats say "port," and all barmaids say "port wine." The whole thing is rather more trivial than collecting tram-tickets; and I will not pursue Lady Grove's further distinctions. I pass over the interesting theory that I ought to say to Jones (even apparently if he is my dearest friend), "How is Mrs. Jones?" instead of "How is your wife?" and I pass over an impassioned declamation about bedspreads (I think) which has failed to fire my blood.

The truth of the matter is really quite simple. An aristocracy is a secret society; and this is especially so when, as in the modern world, it is practically a plutocracy. The one idea of a secret society is to change the password. Lady Grove falls naturally into a pure perversity because she feels subconsciously that the people of England can be more effectively kept at a distance by a perpetual torrent of new tests than by the persistence of a few old ones. She knows that in the educated "middle class" there is an idea that it is vulgar to say port wine; therefore she reverses the idea—she says that the man who would say "port" is a man who would say, "How is your wife?" She says it because she knows both these remarks to be quite obvious and reasonable.

The only thing to be done or said in reply, I suppose, would be to apply the same principle of bold mystification on our own part. I do not see why I should not write a book called "Etiquette in Fleet Street," and terrify every one else out of that thoroughfare by mysterious allusions to the mistakes that they generally make. I might say: "This is the kind of man who would wear a green tie when he went into a tobacconist's," or "You don't see anything wrong in drinking a Benedictine on Thursday?.... No, of course _you_ wouldn't." I might asseverate with passionate disgust and disdain: "The man who is capable of writing sonnets as well as triolets is capable of climbing an omnibus while holding an umbrella." It seems a simple method; if ever I should master it perhaps I may govern England.

THE "EATANSWILL GAZETTE."

The other day some one presented me with a paper called the _Eatanswill Gazette_. I need hardly say that I could not have been more startled if I had seen a coach coming down the road with old Mr. Tony Weller on the box. But, indeed, the case is much more extraordinary than that would be. Old Mr. Weller was a good man, a specially and seriously good man, a proud father, a very patient husband, a sane moralist, and a reliable ally. One could not be so very much surprised if somebody pretended to be Tony Weller. But the _Eatanswill Gazette_ is definitely depicted in "Pickwick" as a dirty and unscrupulous rag, soaked with slander and nonsense. It was really interesting to find a modern paper proud to take its name. The case cannot be compared to anything so simple as a resurrection of one of the "Pickwick" characters; yet a very good parallel could easily be found. It is almost exactly as if a firm of solicitors were to open their offices to-morrow under the name of Dodson and Fogg.

47

It was at once apparent, of course, that the thing was a joke. But what was not apparent, what only grew upon the mind with gradual wonder and terror, was the fact that it had its serious side. The paper is published in the well-known town of Sudbury, in Suffolk. And it seems that there is a standing quarrel between Sudbury and the county town of Ipswich as to which was the town described by Dickens in his celebrated sketch of an election. Each town proclaims with passion that it was Eatanswill. If each town proclaimed with passion that it was not Eatanswill, I might be able to understand it. Eatanswill, according to Dickens, was a town alive with loathsome corruption, hypocritical in all its public utterances, and venal in all its votes. Yet, two highly respectable towns compete for the honour of having been this particular cesspool, just as ten cities fought to be the birthplace of Homer. They claim to be its original as keenly as if they were claiming to be the original of More's "Utopia" or Morris's "Earthly Paradise." They grow seriously heated over the matter. The men of Ipswich say warmly, "It must have been our town; for Dickens says it was corrupt, and a more corrupt town than our town you couldn't have met in a month." The men of Sudbury reply with rising passion, "Permit us to tell you, gentlemen, that our town was quite as corrupt as your town any day of the week. Our town was a common nuisance; and we defy our enemies to question it." "Perhaps you will tell us," sneer the citizens of Ipswich, "that your politics were ever as thoroughly filthy as----" "As filthy as anything," answer the Sudbury men, undauntedly. "Nothing in politics could be filthier. Dickens must have noticed how disgusting we were." "And could he have failed to notice," the others reason indignantly, "how disgusting we were? You could smell us a mile off. You Sudbury fellows may think yourselves very fine, but let me tell you that, compared to our city, Sudbury was an honest place." And so the controversy goes on. It seems to me to be a new and odd kind of controversy.

Naturally, an outsider feels inclined to ask why Eatanswill should be either one or the other. As a matter of fact, I fear Eatanswill was every town in the country. It is surely clear that when Dickens described the Eatanswill election he did not mean it as a satire on Sudbury or a satire on Ipswich; he meant it as a satire on England. The Eatanswill election is not a joke against Eatanswill; it is a joke against elections. If the satire is merely local, it practically loses its point; just as the "Circumlocution Office" would lose its point if it were not supposed to be a true sketch of all Government offices; just as the Lord Chancellor in "Bleak House" would lose his point if he were not supposed to be symbolic and representative of all Lord Chancellors. The whole moral meaning would vanish if we supposed that Oliver Twist had got by accident into an exceptionally bad workhouse, or that Mr. Dorrit was in the only debtors' prison that was not well managed. Dickens was making game, not of places, but of methods. He poured all his powerful genius into trying to make the people ashamed of the methods. But he seems only to have succeeded in making people proud of the places. In any case, the controversy is conducted in a truly extraordinary way. No one seems to allow for the fact that, after all, Dickens was writing a novel, and a highly fantastic novel at that. Facts in support of Sudbury or Ipswich are quoted not only from the story itself, which is wild and wandering enough, but even from the yet wilder narratives which incidentally occur in the story, such as Sam Weller's description of how his father, on the way to Eatanswill, tipped all the voters into the canal. This may quite easily be (to begin with) an entertaining tarradiddle of Sam's own invention, told, like many other even more improbable stories, solely to amuse Mr. Pickwick. Yet the champions of these two towns positively ask each other to produce a canal, or to fail for ever in their attempt to prove themselves the most corrupt town in England. As far as I remember, Sam's story of the canal ends with Mr. Pickwick eagerly asking whether everybody was rescued, and Sam solemnly replying that one old gentleman's hat was found, but that he was not sure whether his head was in it. If the canal is to be taken as realistic, why not the hat and the head? If these critics ever find the canal I recommend them to drag it for the body of the old gentleman.

Both sides refuse to allow for the fact that the characters in the story are comic characters. For instance, Mr. Percy Fitzgerald, the eminent student of Dickens, writes to the *Eatanswill Gazette* to say that Sudbury, a small town, could not have been Eatanswill, because one of the candidates speaks of its great manufactures. But obviously one of the candidates would have spoken of its great manufactures if it had had nothing but a row of apple-stalls. One of the candidates might have said that the commerce of Eatanswill eclipsed Carthage, and covered every sea; it would have been quite in the style of Dickens. But when the champion of Sudbury answers him, he does not point out this plain mistake. He answers by making another mistake exactly of the same kind. He says that Eatanswill was not a busy, important place. And his odd reason is that Mrs. Pott said she was dull there. But obviously Mrs. Pott would have said she was dull anywhere. She was setting her cap at Mr. Winkle. Moreover, it was the whole point of her character in any case. Mrs. Pott was that kind of woman. If she had been in Ipswich she would have said that she ought to be in London. If she was in London she would have said that she ought to be in Paris. The first disputant proves Eatanswill grand because a servile candidate calls it grand. The second proves it dull because a discontented woman calls it dull.

The great part of the controversy seems to be conducted in the spirit of highly irrelevant realism.

Sudbury cannot be Eatanswill, because there was a fancy-dress shop at Eatanswill, and there is no record of a fancy-dress shop at Sudbury. Sudbury must be Eatanswill because there were heavy roads outside Eatanswill, and there are heavy roads outside Sudbury. Ipswich cannot be Eatanswill, because Mrs. Leo Hunter's country seat would not be near a big town. Ipswich must be Eatanswill because Mrs. Leo Hunter's country seat would be near a large town. Really, Dickens might have been allowed to take liberties with such things as these, even if he had been mentioning the place by name. If I were writing a story about the town of Limerick, I should take the liberty of introducing a bun-shop without taking a journey to Limerick to see whether there was a bun-shop there. If I wrote a romance about Torquay, I should hold myself free to introduce a house with a green door without having studied a list of all the coloured doors in the town. But if, in order to make it particularly obvious that I had not meant the town for a photograph either of Torquay or Limerick, I had gone out of my way to give the place a wild, fictitious name of my own, I think that in that case I should be justified in tearing my hair with rage if the people of Limerick or Torquay began to argue about bun-shops and green doors. No reasonable man would expect Dickens to be so literal as all that even about Bath or Bury St. Edmunds, which do exist; far less need he be literal about Eatanswill, which didn't exist.

I must confess, however, that I incline to the Sudbury side of the argument. This does not only arise from the sympathy which all healthy people have for small places as against big ones; it arises from some really good qualities in this particular Sudbury publication. First of all, the champions of Sudbury seem to be more open to the sensible and humorous view of the book than the champions of Ipswich—at least, those that appear in this discussion. Even the Sudbury champion, bent on finding realistic clothes, rebels (to his eternal honour) when Mr. Percy Fitzgerald tries to show that Bob Sawyer's famous statement that he was neither Buff nor Blue, "but a sort of plaid," must have been copied from some silly man at Ipswich who said that his politics were "half and half." Anybody might have made either of the two jokes. But it was the whole glory and meaning of Dickens that he confined himself to making jokes that anybody might have made a little better than anybody would have made them.

FAIRY TALES

Some solemn and superficial people (for nearly all very superficial people are solemn) have declared that the fairy-tales are immoral; they base this upon some accidental circumstances or regrettable incidents in the war between giants and boys, some cases in which the latter indulged in unsympathetic deceptions or even in practical jokes. The objection, however, is not only false, but very much the reverse of the facts. The fairy-tales are at root not only moral in the sense of being innocent, but moral in the sense of being didactic, moral in the sense of being moralising. It is all very well to talk of the freedom of fairyland, but there was precious little freedom in fairyland by the best official accounts. Mr. W.B. Yeats and other sensitive modern souls, feeling that modern life is about as black a slavery as ever oppressed mankind (they are right enough there), have especially described elfland as a place of utter ease and abandonment—a place where the soul can turn every way at will like the wind. Science denounces the idea of a capricious God; but Mr. Yeats's school suggests that in that world every one is a capricious god. Mr. Yeats himself has said a hundred times in that sad and splendid literary style which makes him the first of all poets now writing in English (I will not say of all English poets, for Irishmen are familiar with the practice of physical assault), he has, I say, called up a hundred times the picture of the terrible freedom of the fairies, who typify the ultimate anarchy of art—

"Where nobody grows old or weary or wise,
Where nobody grows old or godly or grave."

But, after all (it is a shocking thing to say), I doubt whether Mr. Yeats really knows the real philosophy of the fairies. He is not simple enough; he is not stupid enough. Though I say it who should not, in good sound human stupidity I would knock Mr. Yeats out any day. The fairies like me better than Mr. Yeats; they can take me in more. And I have my doubts whether this feeling of the free, wild spirits on the crest of hill or wave is really the central and simple spirit of folk-lore. I think the poets have made a mistake: because the world of the fairy-tales is a brighter and more varied world than ours, they have fancied it less moral; really it is brighter and more varied because it is more moral. Suppose a man could be born in a modern prison. It is impossible, of course, because nothing human can happen in a modern prison, though it could sometimes in an ancient dungeon. A modern prison is always inhuman, even when it is not inhumane. But suppose a man were born in a modern prison, and grew accustomed to the deadly silence and the disgusting indifference; and suppose he were then suddenly turned loose upon the life and laughter of Fleet Street. He would, of course, think that the literary men in Fleet Street were a free and happy race; yet how sadly, how ironically, is this the reverse of the case! And so again these toiling serfs in Fleet Street, when they catch a glimpse of the fairies, think the fairies are utterly free. But fairies are like journalists in this and many other respects. Fairies and journalists have an apparent gaiety and a delusive beauty. Fairies and journalists seem to be lovely and lawless; they seem to be both of them too exquisite to descend to the ugliness of everyday duty. But it is an illusion created by the sudden sweetness of their presence. Journalists live under law; and so in fact does fairyland.

If you really read the fairy-tales, you will observe that one idea runs from one end of them to the other—the idea that peace and happiness can only exist on some condition. This idea, which is the core of ethics, is the core of the nursery-tales. The whole happiness of fairyland hangs upon a thread, upon one thread. Cinderella may have a dress woven on supernatural looms and blazing with unearthly brilliance; but she must be back when the clock strikes twelve. The king may invite fairies to the christening, but he must invite all the fairies or frightful results will follow. Bluebeard's wife may open all doors but one. A promise is broken to a cat, and the whole world goes wrong. A promise is broken to a yellow dwarf, and the whole world goes wrong. A girl may be the bride of the God of Love himself if she never tries to see him; she sees him, and he vanishes away. A girl is given a box on condition she does not open it; she opens it, and all the evils of this world rush out at her. A man and woman are put in a garden on condition that they do not eat one fruit: they eat it, and lose their joy in all the fruits of the earth.

This great idea, then, is the backbone of all folk-lore—the idea that all happiness hangs on one thin veto; all positive joy depends on one negative. Now, it is obvious that there are many philosophical and religious ideas akin to or symbolised by this; but it is not with them I wish to deal here. It is surely obvious that all ethics ought to be taught to this fairy-tale tune; that, if one does the thing forbidden, one imperils all the things provided. A man who breaks his promise to his wife ought to be reminded that, even if she is a cat, the case of the fairy-cat shows that such conduct may be incautious. A burglar just about to open some one else's safe should be playfully reminded that he is in the perilous posture of the beautiful Pandora: he is about to lift the forbidden lid and loosen evils unknown. The boy eating some one's apples in some one's apple tree should be a reminder that he has come to a mystical moment of his life, when one apple may rob him of all others. This is the profound morality of fairy-tales; which, so far from being lawless, go to the root of all law. Instead of finding (like common books of ethics) a rationalistic basis for each Commandment, they find the great mystical basis for all Commandments. We are in this fairyland on sufferance; it is not for us to quarrel with the conditions under which we enjoy this wild vision of the world. The vetoes are indeed extraordinary, but then so are the concessions. The idea of property, the idea of some one else's apples, is a rum idea; but then the idea of there being any apples is a rum idea. It is strange and weird that I cannot with safety drink ten bottles of champagne; but then the champagne itself is strange and weird, if you come to that. If I have drunk of the fairies' drink it is but just I should drink by the fairies' rules. We may not see the direct logical connection between three beautiful silver spoons and a large ugly policeman; but then who in fairy tales ever could see the direct logical connection between three bears and a giant, or between a rose and a roaring beast? Not only can these fairy-tales be enjoyed because they are moral, but morality can be enjoyed because it puts us in fairyland, in a world at once of wonder and of war.

TOM JONES AND MORALITY

The two hundredth anniversary of Henry Fielding is very justly celebrated, even if, as far as can be discovered, it is only celebrated by the newspapers. It would be too much to expect that any such merely chronological incident should induce the people who write about Fielding to read him; this kind of neglect is only another name for glory. A great classic means a man whom one can praise without having read. This is not in itself wholly unjust; it merely implies a certain respect for the realisation and fixed conclusions of the mass of mankind. I have never read Pindar (I mean I have never read the Greek Pindar; Peter Pindar I have read all right), but the mere fact that I have not read Pindar, I think, ought not to prevent me and certainly would not prevent me from talking of "the masterpieces of Pindar," or of "great poets like Pindar or Æschylus." The very learned men are angularly unenlightened on this as on many other subjects; and the position they take up is really quite unreasonable. If any ordinary journalist or man of general reading alludes to Villon or to Homer, they consider it a quite triumphant sneer to say to the man, "You cannot read mediæval French," or "You cannot read Homeric Greek." But it is not a triumphant sneer—or, indeed, a sneer at all. A man has got as much right to employ in his speech the established and traditional facts of human history as he has to employ any other piece of common human information. And it is as reasonable for a man who knows no French to assume that Villon was a good poet as it would be for a man who has no ear for music to assume that Beethoven was a good musician. Because he himself has no ear for music, that is no reason why he should assume that the human race has no ear for music. Because I am ignorant (as I am), it does not follow that I ought to assume that I am deceived. The man who would not praise Pindar unless he had read him would be a low, distrustful fellow, the worst kind of sceptic, who doubts not only God, but man. He would be like a man who could not call Mount Everest high unless he had climbed it. He would be like a man who would not admit that the North Pole was cold until he had been there.

But I think there is a limit, and a highly legitimate limit, to this process. I think a man may praise Pindar without knowing the top of a Greek letter from the bottom. But I think that if a man is going to abuse Pindar, if he is going to denounce, refute, and utterly expose Pindar, if he is going to show Pindar up as the utter ignoramus and outrageous impostor that he is, then I think it will be just as well perhaps—I think, at any rate, it would do no harm—if he did know a little Greek, and even had read a little Pindar. And I think the same situation would be involved if the critic were concerned to point out that Pindar was scandalously immoral, pestilently cynical, or low and beastly in his views of life. When people brought such attacks against the morality of Pindar, I should regret that they could not read Greek; and when they bring such attacks against the morality of Fielding, I regret very much that they cannot read English.

There seems to be an extraordinary idea abroad that Fielding was in some way an immoral or offensive writer. I have been astounded by the number of the leading articles, literary articles, and other articles written about him just now in which there is a curious tone of apologising for the man. One critic says that after all he couldn't help it, because he lived in the eighteenth century; another says that we must allow for the change of manners and ideas; another says that he was not altogether without generous and humane feelings; another suggests that he clung feebly, after all, to a few of the less important virtues. What on earth does all this mean? Fielding described Tom Jones as going on in a certain way, in which, most unfortunately, a very large number of young men do go on. It is unnecessary to say that Henry Fielding knew that it was an unfortunate way of going on. Even Tom Jones knew that. He said in so many words that it was a very unfortunate way of going on; he said, one may almost say, that it had ruined his life; the passage is there for the benefit of any one who may take the trouble to read the book. There is ample evidence (though even this is of a mystical and indirect kind), there is ample evidence that Fielding probably thought that it was better to be Tom Jones than to be an utter coward and sneak. There is simply not one rag or thread or speck of evidence to show that Fielding thought that it was better to be Tom Jones than to be a good man. All that he is concerned with is the description of a definite and very real type of young man; the young man whose passions and whose selfish necessities sometimes seemed to be stronger than anything else in him.

The practical morality of Tom Jones is bad, though not so bad, *spiritually* speaking, as the practical morality of Arthur Pendennis or the practical morality of Pip, and certainly nothing like so bad as the profound practical immorality of Daniel Deronda. The practical morality of Tom Jones is bad; but I cannot see any proof that his theoretical morality was particularly bad. There is no need to tell the majority of modern young men even to live up to the theoretical ethics of Henry Fielding. They would suddenly spring into the stature of archangels if they lived up to the theoretic ethics of poor Tom Jones. Tom Jones is still alive, with all his good and all his evil; he is walking about the streets; we meet him every day. We meet with him, we drink with him, we smoke with him, we talk with him, we talk about him. The only difference is that we have no longer the intellectual courage to write about him. We split up the supreme and central human being, Tom Jones, into a number of separate aspects. We let Mr. J.M. Barrie write about him in his good moments, and make him out better than he is. We let Zola write about him in his bad moments, and make him out much worse than he is. We let Maeterlinck celebrate those moments of spiritual panic which he knows to be cowardly; we let Mr. Rudyard Kipling celebrate those moments of brutality which he knows to be far more cowardly. We let obscene writers write about the obscenities of this ordinary man. We let puritan writers write about the purities of this ordinary man. We look through one peephole that makes men out as devils, and we call it the new art. We look through another peephole that makes men out as angels, and we call it the New Theology. But if we pull down some dusty old books from the bookshelf, if we turn over some old mildewed leaves, and if in that obscurity and decay we find some faint traces of a tale about a complete man, such a man as is walking on the pavement outside, we suddenly pull a long face, and we call it the coarse morals of a bygone age.

The truth is that all these things mark a certain change in the general view of morals; not, I think, a change for the better. We have grown to associate morality in a book with a kind of optimism and prettiness; according to us, a moral book is a book about moral people. But the old idea was almost exactly the opposite; a moral book was a book about immoral people. A moral book was full of pictures like Hogarth's "Gin Lane" or "Stages of Cruelty," or it recorded, like the popular broadsheet, "God's dreadful judgment" against some blasphemer or murderer. There is a philosophical reason for this change. The homeless scepticism of our time has reached a sub-conscious feeling that morality is somehow merely a matter of human taste—an accident of psychology. And if goodness only exists in certain human minds, a man wishing to praise goodness will naturally exaggerate the amount of it that there is in human minds or the number of human minds in which it is supreme. Every confession that man is vicious is a confession that virtue is visionary. Every book which admits that evil is real is felt in some vague way to be admitting that good is unreal. The modern instinct is that if the heart of man is evil, there is nothing that remains good. But the older feeling was that if the heart of man was ever so evil, there was something that remained good—goodness remained good. An actual avenging virtue existed outside the human race; to that men rose, or from that men fell away. Therefore, of course, this law itself was as much demonstrated in the breach as in the observance. If Tom Jones violated morality, so much the worse for Tom Jones. Fielding did not feel, as a melancholy modern would have done, that every sin of Tom Jones was in some way breaking the spell, or we may even say destroying the fiction of morality. Men spoke of the sinner breaking the law; but it was rather the law that broke him. And what modern people call the foulness and freedom of Fielding is generally the severity and moral stringency of Fielding. He would not have thought that he was serving morality at all if he had written a book all about nice people. Fielding would have considered Mr. Ian Maclaren extremely immoral; and there is something to be said for that view. Telling the truth about the terrible struggle of the human soul is surely a very elementary part of the ethics of honesty. If the characters are not wicked, the book is. This older and firmer conception of right as existing outside human weakness and without reference to human error can be felt in the very lightest and loosest of the works of old English literature. It is commonly unmeaning enough to call Shakspere a great moralist; but in this particular way Shakspere is a very typical moralist. Whenever he alludes to right and wrong it is always with this old implication. Right is right, even if nobody does it. Wrong is wrong, even if everybody is wrong about it.

THE MAID OF ORLEANS

A considerable time ago (at far too early an age, in fact) I read Voltaire's "La Pucelle," a savage sarcasm on the traditional purity of Joan of Arc, very dirty, and very funny. I had not thought of it again for years, but it came back into my mind this morning because I began to turn over the leaves of the new "Jeanne d'Arc," by that great and graceful writer, Anatole France. It is written in a tone of tender sympathy, and a sort of sad reverence; it never loses touch with a noble tact and courtesy, like that of a gentleman escorting a peasant girl through the modern crowd. It is invariably respectful to Joan, and even respectful to her religion. And being myself a furious admirer of Joan the Maid, I have reflectively compared the two methods, and I come to the conclusion that I prefer Voltaire's.

When a man of Voltaire's school has to explode a saint or a great religious hero, he says that such a person is a common human fool, or a common human fraud. But when a man like Anatole France has to explode a saint, he explains a saint as somebody belonging to his particular fussy little literary set. Voltaire read human nature into Joan of Arc, though it was only the brutal part of human nature. At least it was not specially Voltaire's nature. But M. France read M. France's nature into Joan of Arc—all the cold kindness, all the homeless sentimental sin of the modern literary man. There is one book that it recalled to me with startling vividness, though I have not seen the matter mentioned anywhere; Renan's "Vie de Jésus." It has just the same general intention: that if you do not attack Christianity, you can at least patronise it. My own instinct, apart from my opinions, would be quite the other way. If I disbelieved in Christianity, I should be the loudest blasphemer in Hyde Park. Nothing ought to be too big for a brave man to attack; but there are some things too big for a man to patronise.

And I must say that the historical method seems to me excessively unreasonable. I have no knowledge of history, but I have as much knowledge of reason as Anatole France. And, if anything is irrational, it seems to me that the Renan-France way of dealing with miraculous stories is irrational. The Renan-France method is simply this: you explain supernatural stories that have some foundation simply by inventing natural stories that have no foundation. Suppose that you are confronted with the statement that Jack climbed up the beanstalk into the sky. It is perfectly philosophical to reply that you do not think he did. It is (in my opinion) even more philosophical to reply that he may very probably have done so. But the Renan-France method is to write like this: "When we consider Jack's curious and even perilous heredity, which no doubt was derived from a female greengrocer and a profligate priest, we can easily understand how the ideas of heaven and a beanstalk came to be combined in his mind. Moreover, there is little doubt that he must have met some wandering conjurer from India, who told him about the tricks of the mango plant, and how t is sent up to the sky. We can imagine these two friends, the old man and the young, wandering in the woods together at evening, looking at the red and level clouds, as on that night when the old man pointed to a small beanstalk, and told his too imaginative companion that this also might be made to scale the heavens. And then, when we remember the quite exceptional psychology of Jack, when we remember how there was in him a union of the prosaic, the love of plain vegetables, with an almost irrelevant eagerness for the unattainable, for invisibility and the void, we shall no longer wonder that it was to him especially that was sent this sweet, though merely symbolic, dream of the tree uniting earth and heaven." That is the way that Renan and France write, only they do it better. But, really, a rationalist like myself becomes a little impatient and feels inclined to say, "But, hang it all, what do you know about the heredity of Jack or the psychology of Jack? You know nothing about Jack at all, except that some people say that he climbed up a beanstalk. Nobody would ever have thought of mentioning him if he hadn't. You must interpret him in terms of the beanstalk religion; you cannot merely interpret religion in terms of him. We have the materials of this story, and we can believe them or not. But we have not got the materials to make another story."

It is no exaggeration to say that this is the manner of M. Anatole France in dealing with Joan of Arc. Because her miracle is incredible to his somewhat old-fashioned materialism, he does not therefore dismiss it and her to fairyland with Jack and the Beanstalk. He tries to invent a real story, for which he can find no real evidence. He produces a scientific explanation which is quite destitute of any scientific proof. It is as if I (being entirely ignorant of botany and chemistry) said that the beanstalk grew to the sky because nitrogen and argon got into the subsidiary ducts of the corolla. To take the most obvious example, the principal character in M. France's story is a person who never existed at all. All Joan's wisdom and energy, it seems, came from a certain priest, of whom there is not the tiniest trace in all the multitudinous records of her life. The only foundation I can find for this fancy is the highly undemocratic idea that a peasant girl could not possibly have any ideas of her own. It is very hard for a freethinker to remain democratic. The writer seems altogether to forget what is meant by the moral atmosphere of a community. To say that Joan must have learnt her vision of a virgin overthrowing evil from *a* priest, is like saying that some modern girl in London, pitying the poor, must have learnt it from *a* Labour Member. She would learn it where the Labour Member learnt it—in the whole state of our society.

But that is the modern method: the method of the reverent sceptic. When you find a life entirely incredible and incomprehensible from the outside, you pretend that you understand the inside. As Renan, the rationalist, could not make any sense out of Christ's most public acts, he proceeded to make an ingenious system out of His private thoughts. As Anatole France, on his own intellectual principle, cannot believe in what Joan of Arc did, he professes to be her dearest friend, and to know exactly what she meant. I cannot feel it to be a very rational manner of writing history; and sooner or later we shall have to find some more solid way of dealing with those spiritual phenomena with which all history is as closely spotted and spangled as the sky is with stars.

Joan of Arc is a wild and wonderful thing enough, but she is much saner than most of her critics and biographers. We shall not recover the common sense of Joan until we have recovered her mysticism. Our wars fail, because they begin with something sensible and obvious—such as getting to Pretoria by Christmas. But her war succeeded—because it began with something wild and perfect—the saints delivering France. She put her idealism in the right place, and her realism also in the right place: we moderns get both displaced. She put her dreams and her sentiment into her aims, where they ought to be; she put her practicality into her practice. In modern Imperial wars, the case is reversed. Our dreams, our aims are always, we insist, quite practical. It is our practice that is dreamy.

It is not for us to explain this flaming figure in terms of our tired and querulous culture. Rather we must try to explain ourselves by the blaze of such fixed stars. Those who called her a witch hot from hell were much more sensible than those who depict her as a silly sentimental maiden prompted by her parish priest. If I have to choose between the two schools of her scattered enemies, I could take my place with those subtle clerks who thought her divine mission devilish, rather than with those rustic aunts and uncles who thought it impossible.

A DEAD POET

With Francis Thompson we lose the greatest poetic energy since Browning. His energy was of somewhat the same kind. Browning was intellectually intricate because he was morally simple. He was too simple to explain himself; he was too humble to suppose that other people needed any explanation. But his real energy, and the real energy of Francis Thompson, was best expressed in the fact that both poets were at once fond of immensity and also fond of detail. Any common Imperialist can have large ideas so long as he is not called upon to have small ideas also. Any common scientific philosopher can have small ideas so long as he is not called upon to have large ideas as well. But great poets use the telescope and also the microscope. Great poets are obscure for two opposite reasons; now, because they are talking about something too large for any one to understand, and now again because they are talking about something too small for any one to see. Francis Thompson possessed both these infinities. He escaped by being too small, as the microbe escapes; or he escaped by being too large, as the universe escapes. Any one who knows Francis Thompson's poetry knows quite well the truth to which I refer. For the benefit of any person who does not know it, I may mention two cases taken from memory. I have not the book by me, so I can only render the poetical passages in a clumsy paraphrase. But there was one poem of which the image was so vast that it was literally difficult for a time to take it in; he was describing the evening earth with its mist and fume and fragrance, and represented the whole as rolling upwards as a smoke; then suddenly he called the whole ball of the earth a thurible, and said that some gigantic spirit swung it slowly before God. That is the case of the image too large for comprehension. Another instance sticks in my mind of the image which is too small. In one of his poems, he says that abyss between the known and the unknown is bridged by "Pontifical death." There are about ten historical and theological puns in that one word. That a priest means a pontiff, that a pontiff means a bridge-maker, that death is certainly a bridge, that death may turn out after all to be a reconciling priest, that at least priests and bridges both attest to the fact that one thing can get separated from another thing—these ideas, and twenty more, are all actually concentrated in the word "pontifical." In Francis Thompson's poetry, as in the poetry of the universe, you can work infinitely out and out, but yet infinitely in and in. These two infinities are the mark of greatness; and he was a great poet.

Beneath the tide of praise which was obviously due to the dead poet, there is an evident undercurrent of discussion about him; some charges of moral weakness were at least important enough to be authoritatively contradicted in the *Nation*; and, in connection with this and other things, there has been a continuous stir of comment upon his attraction to and gradual absorption in Catholic theological ideas. This question is so important that I think it ought to be considered and understood even at the present time. It is, of course, true that Francis Thompson devoted himself more and more to poems not only purely Catholic, but, one may say, purely ecclesiastical. And it is, moreover, true that (if things go on as they are going on at present) more and more good poets will do the same. Poets will tend towards Christian orthodoxy for a perfectly plain reason; because it is about the simplest and freest thing now left in the world. On this point it is very necessary to be clear. When people impute special vices to the Christian Church, they seem entirely to forget that the world (which is the only other thing there is) has these vices much more. The Church has been cruel; but the world has been much more cruel. The Church has plotted; but the world has plotted much more. The Church has been superstitious; but it has never been so superstitious as the world is when left to itself.

Now, poets in our epoch will tend towards ecclesiastical religion strictly because it is just a little more free than anything else. Take, for instance, the case of symbol and ritualism. All reasonable men believe in symbol; but some reasonable men do not believe in ritualism; by which they mean, I imagine, a symbolism too complex, elaborate, and mechanical. But whenever they talk of ritualism they always seem to mean the ritualism of the Church. Why should they not mean the ritual of the world? It is much more ritualistic. The ritual of the Army, the ritual of the Navy, the ritual of the Law Courts, the ritual of Parliament are much more ritualistic. The ritual of a dinner-party is much more ritualistic. Priests may put gold and great jewels on the chalice; but at least there is only one chalice to put them on. When you go to a dinner-party they put in front of you five different chalices, of five weird and heraldic shapes, to symbolise five different kinds of wine; an insane extension of ritual from which Mr. Percy Dearmer would fly shrieking. A bishop wears a mitre; but he is not thought more or less of a bishop according to whether you can see the very latest curves in his mitre. But a swell is thought more or less of a swell according to whether you can see the very latest curves in his hat. There is more *fuss* about symbols in the world than in the Church.

And yet (strangely enough) though men fuss more about the worldly symbols, they mean less by them. It is the mark of religious forms that they declare something unknown. But it is the mark of worldly forms that they declare something which is known, and which is known to be untrue. When the Pope in an Encyclical calls himself your father, it is a matter of faith or of doubt. But when the Duke of Devonshire in a letter calls himself yours obediently, you know that he means the opposite of what he says. Religious forms are, at the worst, fables; they might be true. Secular forms are falsehoods; they are not true. Take a more topical case. The German Emperor has more uniforms than the Pope. But, moreover, the Pope's vestments all imply a claim to be something purely mystical and doubtful. Many of the German Emperor's uniforms imply a claim to be something which he certainly is not and which it would be highly disgusting if he were. The Pope may or may not be the Vicar of Christ. But the Kaiser certainly is not an English Colonel. If the thing were reality it would be treason. If it is mere ritual, it is by far the most unreal ritual on earth.

Now, poetical people like Francis Thompson will, as things stand, tend away from secular society and towards religion for the reason above described: that there are crowds of symbols in both, but that those of religion are simpler and mean more. To take an evident type, the Cross is more poetical than the Union Jack, because it is simpler. The more simple an idea is, the more it is fertile in variations. Francis Thompson could have written any number of good poems on the Cross, because it is a primary symbol. The number of poems which Mr. Rudyard Kipling could write on the Union Jack is, fortunately, limited, because the Union Jack is too complex to produce luxuriance. The same principle applies to any possible number of cases. A poet like Francis Thompson could deduce perpetually rich and branching meanings out of two plain facts like bread and wine; with bread and wine he can expand everything to everywhere. But with a French menu he cannot expand anything; except perhaps himself. Complicated ideas do not produce any more ideas. Mongrels do not breed. Religious ritual attracts because there is some sense in it. Religious imagery, so far from being subtle, is the only simple thing left for poets. So far from being merely superhuman, it is the only human thing left for human beings.

CHRISTMAS

There is no more dangerous or disgusting habit than that of celebrating Christmas before it comes, as I am doing in this article. It is the very essence of a festival that it breaks upon one brilliantly and abruptly, that at one moment the great day is not and the next moment the great day is. Up to a certain specific instant you are feeling ordinary and sad; for it is only Wednesday. At the next moment your heart leaps up and your soul and body dance together like lovers; for in one burst and blaze it has become Thursday. I am assuming (of course) that you are a worshipper of Thor, and that you celebrate his day once a week, possibly with human sacrifice. If, on the other hand, you are a modern Christian Englishman, you hail (of course) with the same explosion of gaiety the appearance of the English Sunday. But I say that whatever the day is that is to you festive or symbolic, it is essential that there should be a quite clear black line between it and the time going before. And all the old wholesome customs in connection with Christmas were to the effect that one should not touch or see or know or speak of something before the actual coming of Christmas Day. Thus, for instance, children were never given their presents until the actual coming of the appointed hour. The presents were kept tied up in brown-paper parcels, out of which an arm of a doll or the leg of a donkey sometimes accidentally stuck. I wish this principle were adopted in respect of modern Christmas ceremonies and publications. Especially it ought to be observed in connection with what are called the Christmas numbers of magazines. The editors of the magazines bring out their Christmas numbers so long before the time that the reader is more likely to be still lamenting for the turkey of last year than to have seriously settled down to a solid anticipation of the turkey which is to come. Christmas numbers of magazines ought to be tied up in brown paper and kept for Christmas Day. On consideration, I should favour the editors being tied up in brown paper. Whether the leg or arm of an editor should ever be allowed to protrude I leave to individual choice.

Of course, all this secrecy about Christmas is merely sentimental and ceremonial; if you do not like what is sentimental and ceremonial, do not celebrate Christmas at all. You will not be punished if you don't; also, since we are no longer ruled by those sturdy Puritans who won for us civil and religious liberty, you will not even be punished if you do. But I cannot understand why any one should bother about a ceremonial except ceremonially. If a thing only exists in order to be graceful, do it gracefully or do not do it. If a thing only exists as something professing to be solemn, do it solemnly or do not do it. There is no sense in doing it slouchingly; nor is there even any liberty. I can understand the man who takes off his hat to a lady because it is the customary symbol. I can understand him, I say; in fact, I know him quite intimately. I can also understand the man who refuses to take off his hat to a lady, like the old Quakers, because he thinks that a symbol is superstition. But what point would there be in so performing an arbitrary form of respect that it was not a form of respect? We respect the gentleman who takes off his hat to the lady; we respect the fanatic who will not take off his hat to the lady. But what should we think of the man who kept his hands in his pockets and asked the lady to take his hat off for him because he felt tired?

This is combining insolence and superstition; and the modern world is full of the strange combination. There is no mark of the immense weak-mindedness of modernity that is more striking than this general disposition to keep up old forms, but to keep them up informally and feebly. Why take something which was only meant to be respectful and preserve it disrespectfully? Why take something which you could easily abolish as a superstition and carefully perpetuate it as a bore? There have been many instances of this half-witted compromise. Was it not true, for instance, that the other day some mad American was trying to buy Glastonbury Abbey and transfer it stone by stone to America? Such things are not only illogical, but idiotic. There is no particular reason why a pushing American financier should pay respect to Glastonbury Abbey at all. But if he is to pay respect to Glastonbury Abbey, he must pay respect to Glastonbury. If it is a matter of sentiment, why should he spoil the scene? If it is not a matter of sentiment, why should he ever have visited the scene? To call this kind of thing Vandalism is a very inadequate and unfair description. The Vandals were very sensible people. They did not believe in a religion, and so they insulted it; they did not see any use for certain buildings, and so they knocked them down. But they were not such fools as to encumber their march with the fragments of the edifice they had themselves spoilt. They were at least superior to the modern American mode of reasoning. They did not desecrate the stones because they held them sacred.

Another instance of the same illogicality I observed the other day at some kind of "At Home." I saw what appeared to be a human being dressed in a black evening-coat, black dress-waistcoat, and black dress-trousers, but with a shirt-front made of Jaegar wool. What can be the sense of this sort of thing? If a man thinks hygiene more important than convention (a selfish and heathen view, for the beasts that perish are more hygienic than man, and man is only above them because he is more conventional), if, I say, a man thinks that hygiene is more important than convention, what on earth is there to oblige him to wear a shirt-front at all? But to take a costume of which the only conceivable cause or advantage is that it is a sort of uniform, and then not wear it in the uniform way—this is to be neither a Bohemian nor a gentleman. It is a foolish affectation, I think, in an English officer of the Life Guards never to wear his uniform if he can help it. But it would be more foolish still if he showed himself about town in a scarlet coat and a Jaeger breast-plate. It is the custom nowadays to have Ritual Commissions and Ritual Reports to make rather unmeaning compromises in the ceremonial of the Church of England. So perhaps we shall have an ecclesiastical compromise by which all the Bishops shall wear Jaeger copes and Jaeger mitres. Similarly the King might insist on having a Jaeger crown. But I do not think he will, for he understands the logic of the matter better than that. The modern monarch, like a reasonable fellow, wears his crown as seldom as he can; but if he does it at all, then the only point of a crown is that it is a crown. So let me assure the unknown gentleman in the woollen vesture that the only point of a white shirt-front is that it is a white shirt-front. Stiffness may be its impossible defect; but it is certainly its only possible merit.

Let us be consistent, therefore, about Christmas, and either keep customs or not keep them. If you do not like sentiment and symbolism, you do not like Christmas; go away and celebrate something else; I should suggest the birthday of Mr. M'Cabe. No doubt you could have a sort of scientific Christmas with a hygienic pudding and highly instructive presents stuffed into a Jaeger stocking; go and have it then. If you like those things, doubtless you are a good sort of fellow, and your intentions are excellent. I have no doubt that you are really interested in humanity; but I cannot think that humanity will ever be much interested in you. Humanity is unhygienic from its very nature and beginning. It is so much an exception in Nature that the laws of Nature really mean nothing to it. Now Christmas is attacked also on the humanitarian ground. Ouida called it a feast of slaughter and gluttony. Mr. Shaw suggested that it was invented by poulterers. That should be considered before it becomes more considerable.

I do not know whether an animal killed at Christmas has had a better or a worse time than it would have had if there had been no Christmas or no Christmas dinners. But I do know that the fighting and suffering brotherhood to which I belong and owe everything, Mankind, would have a much worse time if there were no such thing as Christmas or Christmas dinners. Whether the turkey which Scrooge gave to Bob Cratchit had experienced a lovelier or more melancholy career than that of less attractive turkeys is a subject upon which I cannot even conjecture. But that Scrooge was better for giving the turkey and Cratchit happier for getting it I know as two facts, as I know that I have two feet. What life and death may be to a turkey is not my business; but the soul of Scrooge and the body of Cratchit are my business. Nothing shall induce me to darken human homes, to destroy human festivities, to insult human gifts and human benefactions for the sake of some hypothetical knowledge which Nature curtained from our eyes. We men and women are all in the same boat, upon a stormy sea. We owe to each other a terrible and tragic loyalty. If we catch sharks for food, let them be killed most mercifully; let any one who likes love the sharks, and pet the sharks, and tie ribbons round their necks and give them sugar and teach them to dance. But if once a man suggests that a shark is to be valued against a sailor, or that the poor shark might be permitted to bite off a nigger's leg occasionally; then I would court-martial the man—he is a traitor to the ship.

And while I take this view of humanitarianism of the anti-Christmas kind, it is cogent to say that I am a strong anti-vivisectionist. That is, if there is any vivisection, I am against it. I am against the cutting-up of conscious dogs for the same reason that I am in favour of the eating of dead turkeys. The connection may not be obvious; but that is because of the strangely unhealthy condition of modern thought. I am against cruel vivisection as I am against a cruel anti-Christmas asceticism, because they both involve the upsetting of existing fellowships and the shocking of normal good feelings for the sake of something that is intellectual, fanciful, and remote. It is not a human thing, it is not a humane thing, when you see a poor woman staring hungrily at a bloater, to think, not of the obvious feelings of the woman, but of the unimaginable feelings of the deceased bloater. Similarly, it is not human, it is not humane, when you look at a dog to think about what theoretic discoveries you might possibly make if you were allowed to bore a hole in his head. Both the humanitarians' fancy about the feelings concealed inside the bloater, and the vivisectionists' fancy about the knowledge concealed inside the dog, are unhealthy fancies, because they upset a human sanity that is certain for the sake of something that is of necessity uncertain. The vivisectionist, for the sake of doing something that may or may not be useful, does something that certainly is horrible. The anti-Christmas humanitarian, in seeking to have a sympathy with a turkey which no man can have with a turkey, loses the sympathy he has already with the happiness of millions of the poor.

It is not uncommon nowadays for the insane extremes in reality to meet. Thus I have always felt that brutal Imperialism and Tolstoian non-resistance were not only not opposite, but were the same thing. They are the same contemptible thought that conquest cannot be resisted, looked at from the two standpoints of the conqueror and the conquered. Thus again teetotalism and the really degraded gin-selling and dram-drinking have exactly the same moral philosophy. They are both based on the idea that fermented liquor is not a drink, but a drug. But I am specially certain that the extreme of vegetarian humanity is, as I have said, akin to the extreme of scientific cruelty—they both permit a dubious speculation to interfere with their ordinary charity. The sound moral rule in such matters as vivisection always presents itself to me in this way. There is no ethical necessity more essential and vital than this: that casuistical exceptions, though admitted, should be admitted as exceptions. And it follows from this, I think, that, though we may do a horrid thing in a horrid situation, we must be quite certain that we actually and already are in that situation. Thus, all sane moralists admit that one may sometimes tell a lie; but no sane moralist would approve of telling a little boy to practise telling lies, in case he might one day have to tell a justifiable one. Thus, morality has often justified shooting a robber or a burglar. But it would not justify going into the village Sunday school and shooting all the little boys who looked as if they might grow up into burglars. The need may arise; but the need must have arisen. It seems to me quite clear that if you step across this limit you step off a precipice.

Now, whether torturing an animal is or is not an immoral thing, it is, at least, a dreadful thing. It belongs to the order of exceptional and even desperate acts. Except for some extraordinary reason I would not grievously hurt an animal; with an extraordinary reason I would grievously hurt him. If (for example) a mad elephant were pursuing me and my family, and I could only shoot him so that he would die in agony, he would have to die in agony. But the elephant would be there. I would not do it to a hypothetical elephant. Now, it always seems to me that this is the weak point in the ordinary vivisectionist argument, "Suppose your wife were dying." Vivisection is not done by a man whose wife is dying. If it were it might be lifted to the level of the moment, as would be lying or stealing bread, or any other ugly action. But this ugly action is done in cold blood, at leisure, by men who are not sure that it will be of any use to anybody—men of whom the most that can be said is that they may conceivably make the beginnings of some discovery which may perhaps save the life of some one else's wife in some remote future. That is too cold and distant to rob an act of its immediate horror. That is like training the child to tell lies for the sake of some great dilemma that may never come to him. You are doing a cruel thing, but not with enough passion to make it a kindly one.

So much for why I am an anti-vivisectionist; and I should like to say, in conclusion, that all other anti-vivisectionists of my acquaintance weaken their case infinitely by forming this attack on a scientific speciality in which the human heart is commonly on their side, with attacks upon universal human customs in which the human heart is not at all on their side. I have heard humanitarians, for instance, speak of vivisection and field sports as if they were the same kind of thing. The difference seems to me simple and enormous. In sport a man goes into a wood and mixes with the existing life of that wood; becomes a destroyer only in the simple and healthy sense in which all the creatures are destroyers; becomes for one moment to them what they are to him—another animal. In vivisection a man takes a simpler creature and subjects it to subtleties which no one but man could inflict on him, and for which man is therefore gravely and terribly responsible.

Meanwhile, it remains true that I shall eat a great deal of turkey this Christmas; and it is not in the least true (as the vegetarians say) that I shall do it because I do not realise what I am doing, or because I do what I know is wrong, or that I do it with shame or doubt or a fundamental unrest of conscience. In one sense I know quite well what I am doing; in another sense I know quite well that I know not what I do. Scrooge and the Cratchits and I are, as I have said, all in one boat; the turkey and I are, to say the most of it, ships that pass in the night, and greet each other in passing. I wish him well; but it is really practically impossible to discover whether I treat him well. I can avoid, and I do avoid with horror, all special and artificial tormenting of him, sticking pins in him for fun or sticking knives in him for scientific investigation. But whether by feeding him slowly and killing him quickly for the needs of my brethren, I have improved in his own solemn eyes his own strange and separate destiny, whether I have made him in the sight of God a slave or a martyr, or one whom the gods love and who die young—that is far more removed from my possibilities of knowledge than the most abstruse intricacies of mysticism or theology. A turkey is more occult and awful than all the angels and archangels In so far as God has partly revealed to us an angelic world, he has partly told us what an angel means. But God has never told us what a turkey means. And if you go and stare at a live turkey for an hour or two, you will find by the end of it that the enigma has rather increased than diminished.

Made in the USA
Monee, IL
17 February 2023

28112324R00038